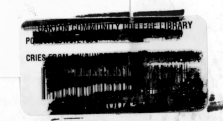

CRIES FROM A
WOUNDED MADRID

CRIES FROM A
WOUNDED MADRID

Poetry of the Spanish Civil War

selected and translated by

CARLOS BAUER

Bilingual Edition

 SWALLOW PRESS   *Athens Ohio   Chicago   London*

Swallow Press books
are published by
Ohio University Press
Athens, Ohio 45701

Library of Congress Cataloging in Publication Data
Main entry under title:

Cries from a wounded Madrid.

   Text in English and Spanish.
   1. Spanish poetry—20th century—Translations into
English. 2. English poetry—Translations from Spanish.
3. Spanish poetry—20th century. 4. Spain—History—
Civil War, 1936–1939—Poetry. 5. War poetry, Spanish.
6. War poetry, Spanish—Translations into English.
7. War poetry, English—Translations from Spanish.
I. Bauer, Carlos.
PQ6267.E5W372   1984   861'.62'08   83-18304
ISBN 0-8040-0421-8
ISBN 0-8040-0376-9 (pbk.)

For Isabel Fuentes Conde, who suffered through this long "mal de las ausencias"

INDICE

CONTENTS

III   *Homenaje de Despedida a las Brigadas Internacionales*

Contents

III Farewell Homage to the International Brigades

I would like to thank the following people for their help in preparing this book: the poets Julián Marcos, Rafael Lorente, Antonio Leyva; the publishers (and poets) José Esteban and Jesús Munárriz; Isabel Fonseca from the Biblioteca Nacional in Madrid, and the librarians in charge of the Southworth Collection at the University of California at San Diego; Pascual Palacios Tardez, for letting me reproduce his drawing, "Madrid, marzo de 1939"; and finally, my editor, Donna Ippolito.

INTRODUCTION

A young Argentinean woman, caught up in the fervor of the first months of civil war in Spain, expresses the feelings of the vast majority: "The things the government is going to do! You'll see! Agrarian reform, new schools, new teachers, new theater, the museums enlarged, popular libraries, art for the people...."[1]

Clearly, the Spanish Civil War transcended a mere struggle to preserve a democratic government against a cabal of rebellious generals, the fascist Falange and a reactionary clergy. There was also a revolution taking place within the civil war, and a vast cultural revolution within that revolution. While not quite as important as one's daily bread, culture came to be viewed as just one more thing the Spanish people had been deprived of throughout history. And once civil war broke out, the Spanish masses proved to be more starved for culture—and knowledge— than anyone had imagined. Even in the face of the fascist terror, government and intellectuals joined together in responding to those cravings, and they went far beyond what could be considered simplistic "agit-prop." A few examples: "cultural militias" taught more than a hundred thousand Spaniards to read and write, both at the front and behind the lines; *bibliobuses* (trucks and buses made into mobile libraries) took thousands of books and periodicals to the front; the *Altovoz del frente* (Loudspeaker of the Front) brought theater, movies, music and poetry readings into the trenches and—because of their close proximity—into the trenches of Franco's troops as well; painters made reproductions of the most famous works from El Prado so they could be transported to the front lines; national monuments and palaces of historical importance— even the palace of Franco's agent in London, the Duke of Alba—were protected against the fascist bombing and shelling by brigades of volunteer militiamen; army units set up printing presses, many times in the trenches, to publish their own newpapers and other publications. One could go on and on. Culture permeated every aspect of life during the thirty-three months of civil war.

But at the forefront of all this cultural activity stood poetry. As Max Aub wrote; "Spanish poetry was, maybe, the only thing prepared for [the civil war]."[2] With very few exceptions the major poets of the day joined

xi

wholeheartedly in the defense of the Spanish Republic. Younger poets wrote while at the front; older ones worked in government service behind the lines. The writing of poetry, however, was not limited to known poets. Soldiers who had barely learned to read and write would recite their first compositions to their companions in the trenches. When the Republican aviation showered manifestoes and ultimatums on the Francoist forces, a few poems were thrown in for good measure.

Poetry was everywhere. Even the Nationalist side produced vast amounts, and a handful of Nationalist poets (Gerardo Diego and Manuel Machado, for example) did stand out. Also, poetry was written in the other languages of the Spanish Peninsula, most notably in Catalan. The quantity of published poetry is staggering: 15,000 to 20,000 compositions by some 5,000 different authors, three-fourths of which originated in the Republican zone.[3]

Just as my own generation, during the war in Viet Nam, found its voice in the lyrics of rock music, the Spaniard of war-fevered 1936 encountered his voice in the verse forms of the traditional "romance," a basically oral form of epic poetry that consists of short eight-syllable lines employing assonance rather than full rhyme. Spain, probably because of the high rate of illiteracy, never lost its oral poetic tradition. The great popularity achieved by Antonio Machado's verse and Federico García Lorca's *Romancero gitano* in the first third of the twentieth century appear to bear this out. Many of the romances written during the civil war were also set to music and sung in the streets, broadcast over the radio, and even chanted on street corners by the blind who sold lottery tickets. The romance quickly became an oral newsreel of the streets, the cry of a frightened and abandoned people. Throughout the autumn of 1936 the romance reinforced the morale of soldier and civilian alike, and brought the *madrileños* together in common cause against the fascist siege. In November 1936, when the capital appeared ready to fall, when there was only one gun for every three men, an almost unarmed rabble of civilians (brigades of barbers, brigades of bakers...logistics handled by housewife associations) had the propagandistic verse of the romance upon their lips, and it was that verse which gave them the spirit to hold out against wave upon wave of Franco's *legionarios* and Moors, to endure the endless bombardment of German and Italian planes. For that reason, that time will always be remembered as one of the few moments in history when poetry did in fact make a difference.

Though the Republican side published books in great number (until a paper shortage forced them to rely on recycled paper), most poetry appeared in newspapers and magazines. Army units, political parties, unions, professional groups, cultural organizations, some branches of

Introduction

government—all had their own publications. Many of these publications had a special section set aside for war poetry, and it was not uncommon to see a poem by a Rafael Alberti or a Miguel Hernández side by side with a composition by some unknown militiaman, or next to an article that explained how to clean and take care of a rifle. Yet of all the periodicals published during the Spanish Civil War, two stand out: *El Mono Azul* and *Hora de España.*

Founded by the Alliance of Anti-fascist Intellectuals in Madrid at the end of August 1936, *El Mono Azul* (literally "The Blue Overall" of the worker-soldiers who made up the great majority of Republican combatants) is the magazine that best represents the hopes and feelings of the first six months of civil war. It was the magazine most committed to the cause of popular culture, solidarity between worker and intellectual, the strongest proponent of the romance, and the first to open up its pages to all who wished to send in their verse. *El Mono Azul* served as the model for all other periodicals that followed it.

Although the romance was by far the most popular form of poetry throughout the Spanish Civil War, it was not the only type of verse written. Free verse and other forms began to appear after the outburst of emotion—and hope—of the first few months gave way to the realization that the Spanish Civil War would turn out to be a long and bitter conflict. The frustrations and anguishes of this second phase of the war are best exemplified in the poetry published by the magazine *Hora de España* ("Spain's Hour"). Though born in the middle of the civil war, *Hora de España* has long been considered one of the most important literary magazines published in Spain in the twentieth century.

As this anthology is the first attempt at a systematic compilation of Spanish Civil War poetry in English—though some poetry was published during the war years, and a few poems have appeared since—several requirements had to be taken into account: that romances from *El Mono Azul* and poems from *Hora de España* be included; that poetry from the different phases, or moments, of the civil war be represented; and that the poetry be presented in a way which would give the English-speaking reader some feeling of how this material was originally presented to the Spanish public.

Three of the most important anthologies published during the Spanish Civil War fulfill these requirements, so the solution was only one of making selections from them. An effort was also made to conserve the original format as much as possible.

1. *Romancero de la guerra civil (Serie I),* published by the Education Ministry in beleaguered Madrid at the end of November 1936,

collected in one volume some thirty-five romances first published in *El Mono Azul* during those emotion-filled months at the beginning of the civil war.

2. *Poetas in la España leal* was published in July 1937 to commemorate the Second International Congress of Anti-fascist Writers which was held that year in Valencia, Barcelona and Madrid. Among the participants were Malcolm Cowley, W.H. Auden, Steven Spender, Pablo Neruda, César Vallejo, Octavio Paz, André Malraux and Tristan Tzara. Published by the government publishing house Ediciones Españolas, under the direction of the editors of *Hora de España*, this anthology brought together forty-four poems, almost all of which had previously appeared in *Hora de España*.

3. The brief *Homenaje de despedida a las Brigadas Internacionales* (Ediciones Españolas) is a collection of just fourteen poems. Here we have a book that came out in the final months of the war, a book that commemorated one of the last nails in the coffin: the International Brigades' farewell parade in Barcelona at the end of October 1938. That event turned out to be one of the most moving moments of the war. Soldiers of the International Brigades openly wept along with the people of Barcelona who had come to see them depart.

It is always difficult to separate myth from reality, wrench aesthetic from passion: the poetry of the Spanish Civil War seems forever to be condemned to the hazards of human passions and partisan politics. Nobody questions the importance of these three collections as historical documents; but one has to ask: does this poetry transcend the confines of momentary obligations and revolutionary zeal, does it stand the test of time? Could the poet Luis Cernuda be right when he wrote that none of this excessive outpouring of verse survived the conflict?[4] Or are the conclusions of younger scholars (e.g., Natalia Calamai) closer to the truth? Calamai: "After studying the poetic production of the civil war years, it is impossible to come to any other conclusion than that this great artistic richness produced by the Republican zone deserves *not* to be forgotten."[5]

Maybe war is not the best atmosphere for literature—but maybe great poetry, great literature, is sometimes created in spite of the tragic and compelling circumstances into which the poet is thrown.

Perhaps we will never be free of the political implications of the Spanish Civil War, free enough to judge its literature solely by esthetic criteria.

Perhaps all one can do is read these heartfelt, passionate poems and

Introduction

reflect on how Franco would boast of having personally signed a quarter of a million death sentences.

And maybe history should never let us forget the 600,000 who died, or the million thrown into concentration camps and prisons, or the 400,000 forced into exile.

It was in Spain that men learned that one can be right and still be beaten, that force can vanquish spirit, that there are times when courage is not its own reward. It is this, without doubt, which explains why so many men throughout the world regard the Spanish drama as a personal tragedy.

ALBERT CAMUS

CRIES FROM A
WOUNDED MADRID

EDICIONES DE LA GUERRA CIVIL

Altolaguirre, Varela, Aleixandre, Logroño, Herrera
Petere, Pérez Infante, Fernández, Garfias, Bergamín,
Alberti, Dieste, García Luque, Plá y Beltrán, Prados,
Hernández, Boda, Aparicio, Serrano Plaja, Gaya,
Beltrán Logroño, Ruanova, Quiroga Plá.

ROMANCERO DE LA GUERRA CIVIL

(SERIE I)

MINISTERIO DE INSTRUCCIÓN PÚBLICA
Y BELLAS ARTES
SECCIÓN DE PUBLICACIONES
MADRID, NOVIEMBRE 1936

ROMANCES HEROICOS

Romances of the Civil War

(Series I)

Almost from the time the romance appeared in the fourteenth century it has been used for purposes of propaganda. In the poems written during the civil war between Pedro I and Enrique de Trastamara, which ended 1369, there is a clear political content. The new romances of the 1936 Civil War closely follow the form of the medieval ones: the eight-syllable line using assonance continues; the epic narrative, brief and direct, is also conserved; and the new romance, like the traditional one, was written to be sung or recited in public. An attempt was even made to conserve the various types of romances. For example, in the section ROMANCES OF MOORS there is an effort to inject a new content into the ancient romances about Moors and Moriscos of the Reconquest and War of Granada. ROMANCES OF THE DEFENSE OF MADRID is the only exception, being wholly a product of besieged Madrid of 1936.

The language employed by the new romance is direct, concise, simple, almost telegraphic, filled with exclamations and repetition of ideas. These poems recount the deeds of the people's heroes, and the hopes and feelings of the people as a whole. Even geography takes on an importance of its own: Madrid, for example, is as much a protagonist as any one of the people's heroes.

The poets who wrote these new romances were not poetic traditionalists. The aesthetic vanguard abandoned their earlier styles to write romances for and about the people once the Spanish Republic came under attack. Rafael Alberti and Vicente Aleixandre are examples of this commitment. And because of that, these poems remain a testament to a moment in history when poetry did make a difference.

1

ROMANCES HEROICOS

El Fusilado

Veinte años justos tenía
José Lorente Granero
cuando se alistó en las filas
de las Milicias de hierro,
y salió para la Sierra
diciendo sólo: "¡Si vuelvo,
hermanos, será cantando
con vosotros; si no, muerto!"
Y una luz brilló de llamas
en sus grandes ojos negros.
Doce noches con sus días,
luchó José entre los cerros,
bajo una luna de agosto
que endurecía los pechos.
Luchó y mató; un nimbo rojo
iluminaba su cuerpo,
y de las balas traidoras
parecía protegerlo.
Su fusil entre sus manos
era una rosa de fuego
vomitando espanto y muerte
para el enemigo negro.
¡Miradlo erguido en el monte,
hermoso, fuerte y sereno,
héroe entre sus camaradas,
entre las balas ileso!
Mas, ¡ay!, que llegó una noche,
noche de pena y de duelo,
noche de tormenta obscura,
noche de cielo cubierto.
En la refriega, José,
de venganza y furor ebrio,
persiguiendo puso en fuga
a un grupo de hombres siniestros
que escapaban entre breñas
como lobos carniceros.

HEROIC ROMANCES

The One Who Was Shot

Exactly twenty years old
was José Lorente Granero
when he joined the ranks
of the Militias of Iron,
and he left for the Sierra,
saying only: "If I come back,
brothers, it will be singing
with you; if not, then dead!"
And a flaming light shone
in his large black eyes.
Twelve nights, with their days,
among the hills fought José,
and also under an August moon
that filled him with resolve.
He fought and killed; a red
halo illuminated his body,
and it seemed to protect him
from those traitorous bullets.
The gun in his hands
was like a fiery rose,
vomiting death and terror
upon that black enemy.
Look at him proud on the mountain,
handsome, strong and serene,
a hero among his comrades,
unscathed amid the bullets!
But, alas, one night arrived,
night of sorrow and grief,
night of dark storm,
night of clouded skies.
In the skirmish, José,
with vengeance and in a blind rage,
while in pursuit put to flight
a group of sinister men
who were escaping through the brambles
like flesh-eating wolves.

3

Corrió y corrió, corrió tanto
José, solo, persiguiéndolos,
que cuando quiso mirar
atrás con sus ojos negros
no vió sino soledad,
soledad, noche y silencio.
De repente unos traidores,
a docenas si no a cientos,
de sus cubiles brotaron,
de sorpresa le cogieron;
entre todos le rodean,
aunque él tumba a cinco, muertos,
y a insultos, golpes, atado,
le llevan al campamento.
¡Ay, voz que cantas la vida
de este muchacho del pueblo,
honor de la gesta heroica,
José Lorente Granero:
calla y no digas la triste
terminación del suceso
ocurrido entre las peñas
que baña un arroyo fresco!
Contra unas tapias le pone
la turba de bandoleros,
y José los mira a todos
con un altivo desprecio.
Apuntan nueve fusiles
a aquel noble y limpio pecho,
espejo de milicianos
y de valientes espejo,
y del desdén de su boca
un salivazo soberbio
va a aplastarse entre los ojos
del jefe vil fusilero.
¡Que así va a afrontar la muerte
quien tiene temple de acero!
¡Ay, voz que cantas la historia
que aquí escucháis de Granero:
acaba y narra hasta el fin,
maravilloso suceso
ocurrido en una noche
de temeroso recuerdo!

He ran and ran, José, alone,
ran so much pursuing them that
when he tried to look back
with his black eyes
he saw but solitude,
solitude, night and silence.
Suddenly some traitors,
by the dozens if not hundreds,
sprang from their lairs,
taking him by surprise;
together they surround him,
though he lays five out dead,
and with insults, blows, tied-up,
he is carried off to their camp.
Oh, voice that sings about the life
of this lad of the people,
an honor to heroic conduct,
José Lorente Granero:
be silent and do not tell
the sad ending of the incident
that occurred amid the boulders
bathed by a cool stream!
Against some mud walls
the gang of outlaws places him,
and José observes them all
with a proud contempt.
They aim nine guns
at the noble and pure breast,
the model of a militiaman,
and of the brave a model,
and a magnificent gob of spit,
made from the scorn in his mouth,
goes spattering between the eyes
of that vile head rifleman.
For, thus, is he going to face death,
this one who has the temper of steel!
Oh, voice that sings this story
you now are hearing about Granero:
finish and relate to the end
this marvelous event
that occurred in a night
of dreadful remembrance!

5

Sonó aquella voz infame:
¡Fuego!, gritó, y fuego hicieron
las nueve bocas malditas
que plomo vil escupieron,
y nueve balas buscaron
la tierna carne de un pecho
que latió por el amor
y la libertad del pueblo.
Rodó un cuerpo entre las piedras,
reinó un profundo silencio,
sólo roto por los pasos
que se alejaban siniestros.
La tierra sola quedaba.
Sola no: ella y su muerto.

¡Ay, tú, José, que me escuchas,
tendido, solo y sangriento!,
¿quién eres que así no oyes
los miles de roncos pechos
que desde el fondo te llaman
por ríos, valles y cerros?
¿Quién eres que no te alzas
ante el clamoroso imperio
de miles de corazones
con un mismo son latiendo?

Amanecía la aurora
y el alba doraba el cuerpo,
un cuerpo que con el día
se levantó de este suelo,
y en pie, sangrando, terrible,
adelantó el pie derecho
y subió monte hacia arriba,
como un sol que va naciendo
y va dejando su sangre
o su luz como un reguero.

José no murió. ¡Miradlo!
Resucitado, no ha muerto;
que no murió, como no
morirá jamás el pueblo.
Podrán fusiles y balas
pretender herir su pecho.

That disgusting voice rang out.
Fire! it shouted and fire they did,
those nine damned muzzles
which spat out vile lead,
and nine bullets sought out
the tender flesh of a breast
which beat for the love
and the freedom of the people.
A body rolled amid the stones,
a profound silence reigned,
broken only by the footsteps
that were sinisterly departing.
The earth alone remained.
Not alone: she and her dead man.

Alas, you, José, who does hear me,
sprawled out, alone and bloodied!
Who are you that does not hear
the thousands of hoarse breasts
calling out to you from the depths,
over rivers, valleys and hills?
Who are you that does not arise
before this clamorous pride
of thousands of hearts
beating with the same sound?

The dawn began to appear
and the sunrise gilded his body,
a body that with the day
arose from this ground,
and once standing, bloody, terrible,
moved its right foot forward
and went up the mountain
like a sun being born
and goes about leaving its blood
or its light behind in a trickle.

José did not die. Look at him!
Resurrected, he has not died;
he did not die, just as
the people will never die.
Guns and bullets may seek
to wound his breast.

7

Podrán bombas y cañones
intentar romper su cuerpo.
Pero el pueblo vive y vence,
pueblo sin tacha y sin miedo,
que en una aurora de sangre
está como un sol naciendo.

VICENTE ALEIXANDRE

Lina Odena

Por Granada, tropas moras.
Por Málaga, son leales.
Y de Málaga a Granada
es de fieles el viaje.
Por allá va Lina Odena,
donde nunca fuera antes.
Va camino de la muerte,
va dirigiendo el avance.
Por allá va Lina Odena,
donde nunca fuera antes.
Quiere avisarle el vigía
y no puede darle alcance.
El auto que la llevaba
sigue camino adelante.
¡Lina Odena, Lina Odena,
ya nadie puede salvarte!
¡Ya no veremos tu risa,
tu estrella de comandante!
¡Ya tus palabras guerreras
no encenderán nuestra sangre!
¡Qué falsa noticia tienes!
¡De qué camino fiaste!
Carretera envenenada
de negras flechas fatales.
Lina Odena, Lina Odena,
por qué traición te engañaste.
Ya no sonará tu voz
por los soldados leales.

Bombs and cannons may try
to break his body.
But the people live and conquer,
a flawless and fearless people,
that in a bloody dawn
is like a sun being born.

VICENTE ALEIXANDRE

Lina Odena[1]

Around Granada, Moorish troops.
Around Málaga they're loyal.
And from Málaga to Granada
the journey is for our loyal ones.
There goes Lina Odena,
where she never went before.
She's traveling death's route,
going about directing the advance.
There goes Lina Odena,
where she never went before.
The lookout wants to warn her
and isn't able to catch her.
The auto carrying her
continues on its way.
Lina Odena, Lina Odena,
now no one can save you!
No longer will we see your laughter,
your commander's star!
No longer will your warlike words
set our blood aflame!
What false news you possess!
What route to have put your trust in!
Road poisoned
by black, fatal arrows.
Lina Odena, Lina Odena,
why didn't you see the treachery?
No longer will your voice resound
for the Loyalist soldiers.

9

Sólo sonarán tus balas
de justicia en los trigales.
Sólo sonará tu cuerpo
cayendo en los olivares.
Sólo contra las arenas,
a luz sonará tu sangre.
Lina Odena, Lina Odena,
camarada del linaje
claro, de todos los héroes,
que sangrarán por vengarte.
¡Tú caíste, Lina Odena,
pero no tus libertades!
Que de Málaga a Granada,
tierra, trigos y olivares,
y las novias y las madres
no temen ya a criminales.
¡Que de Málaga a Granada
los caminos son leales!
¡Que todo alberga alegrías;
sólo tu muerte, pesares!

LORENZO VARELA

El Tren Blindado

Curvas de retama y piedra,
altos llanos los de Avila,
de polvaredas y vientos,
puño cerrado y metralla,
rotos montes en trinchera,
sierras hendidas, cortadas,
de terraplenes y túneles,
taludes y obras de fábrica.
Puesta de sol de aviones
queda alumbrando la rampa
que el tren blindado atraviesa,
aire rojo, verdes llamas.
Truena la locomotora;
el cañón, en sus entrañas.

Only your bullets of justice
in the wheat fields will resound.
Only your body falling
in the olive groves will resound.
Only against the sands, with
the light, will your blood resound.
Lina Odena, Lina Odena,
comrade of clear lineage,
the same as all the heroes
who will bleed to avenge you.
You did fall, Lina Odena,
but not your freedoms!
For from Málaga to Granada,
earth, wheat and olive groves,
and brides and mothers
now no longer fear criminals.
For from Málaga to Granada
the roads are loyalist!
Now everything harbors joy;
and only your death, sorrows!

LORENZO VARELA

The Armored Train

Curves of broom and stone,
high plains, those of Avila,
with clouds of dust and winds,
closed fists and shrapnel,
mountains broken up into roadbeds,
split and cut up mountain ranges,
with embankments, tunnels,
gradients and factory construction.
A sunset of airplanes
is still illuminating the ramp
the armored train is traveling over,
red air, green flames.
The locomotive thunders;
the cannon, in its bowels.

Un hurancán de explosiones
barre los montes de Avila.
El aire de ardiente pólvora
seca bocas by gargantas;
las baterías del 15
responden a retaguardia.
Ya se acercan los muchachos
del compañero Mangada.
Arellanos y morteros,
bombas Laffite y granadas,
nidos de ametralladoras
enfilan rocas peladas.
Un huracán de explosiones
barre los montes de Avila.
Ya se acercan los muchachos.
¡Venid, bravos camaradas!
El tren blindado atraviesa
los montes y las barrancas,
el tren blindado conquista
para los pobres España.

¡Afuera, turbios negocios,
hambres, miserias y lágrimas!
¡Morid, traidores fascistas,
el tren blindado os aplasta!
Curvas de retama y piedra,
altos llanos los de Avila,
de trabajo y alegría
veréis florecer España
y en letras de acero un ¡Vivan
las Milicias Ferroviarias!

JOSE HERRERA PETERE

José Colom

Por España, por el aire,
vuela el capitán del pueblo,
y ve los ríos de sangre

12

A hurricane of explosions
sweeps over the mountains of Avila.
The burning air of gunpowder
dries mouths and throats;
the batteries of the 15th
reply from the rear guard.
The lads of comrade Mangada
now are getting near.
Arellanos[2] and mortar men,
Laffite bombs and grenades,
nests of machine guns
shower stripped clean rocks.
A hurricane of explosions
sweeps over the mountains of Avila.
Now the lads are getting near.
Come, brave comrades!
The armored train crosses
over mountains and ravines,
the armored train is conquering
Spain for her poor.

Out of here, shady business deals,
hungers, miseries and tears!
Die, traitorous fascists, for
this armored train will crush you!
Curves of broom and stone,
high plains, those of Avila,
for with work and joy
you will see Spain blossom,
and, in letters of steel, one:
Long live the Railroad Militias!

JOSE HERRERA PETERE

José Colom

Around Spain, through the air,
flies the people's captain,
and he sees rivers of blood

13

regando los cementerios;
ríos de sangre, ríos de sangre,
reflejando los incendios.
Todo lo que ve lo mira
con tristeza desde el viento.
Triste, entre nubes, vigila
al enemigo sin miedo.
Si el campo de los rebeldes
parece visión de infierno,
vuelve los ojos y mira
para el campo de los nuestros.
Capitán José Colom,
mira el mapa que te ofrezco:
son las tierras de Levante,
que elevan el pensamiento;
las tierras que tú defiendes
contra moros y extranjeros.
Capitán José Colom,
si lloras yo te comprendo;
si media España está libre,
media sufre cautiverio,
y más te mueven las penas
de los que están prisioneros
que las voces de triunfo,
que las palabras de aliento.
Capitán, mis voces suben
por el aire, por el cielo,
que si estoy fuera de mí
es por conocer los hechos;
que si sufro es porque hablo
tan sólo con tu recuerdo.
Capitán José Colom,
yo sé que estás en tu puesto,
que quien muere como tú
no abandona nuestro Ejército.
Tu nombre glorioso está
firme en las líneas de fuego,
y hazañas como la tuya
son el mejor parapeto
para impedir el avance
del desalmado armamento.
Tú te quedaste sin armas,
pero aún te quedaba el cuerpo,

14

watering the cemeteries;
rivers of blood, rivers of blood,
reflecting the fires upward.
All that he sees he sadly
observes from up in the wind.
Sad, from the clouds he boldly
keeps watch over the enemy.
If the terrain of the rebels
seems a vision of hell,
he turns his eyes and looks
toward our side's terrain.
Captain José Colom,
observe this map I offer you:
these are the lands of Levante,
they make one's thoughts soar,
the lands you're defending
against Moors and foreigners.
Captain José Colom,
if you cry I'll understand;
if half of Spain is free,
half suffers in captivity;
and you're moved more by the sufferings
of those who are prisoners
than by triumphant voices,
than by courageous words.
Captain, my shouts rise up
through the air, through the sky,
for if I am beside myself,
it's for knowing the facts;
if I suffer, it's because I speak
only to your remembrance.
Captain José Colom,
I know you're at your post,
for whoever dies like you
never abandons our Army.
Your glorious name is
resolute on the firing lines,
and feats like yours
are the best rampart
for impeding the advance
of their heartless armament.
You were left without weapons,
but still had your body;

te quedaba tu aeroplano,
y no dudaste un momento
en derribar con tu muerte
al invasor traicionero.
Si sin vida te quedaste,
¡viva siempre tu recuerdo!

MANUEL ALTOLAGUIRRE

El Frío en la Sierra

Malagosto, cumbre recia,
estar quieta te conviene.
Reventón, tus andurriales
sean de tierra caliente.
Lomas de viento de hielo,
sed ya de jardines verdes,
que los soldados del pueblo
no pasen frío en el frente.
Cumbres de brisas heladas,
sujetad aún vuestras nieves.
Nublados de los otoños,
tristes fríos de septiembre,
no hiráis a los milicianos
que pasan noche en el frente.
¡Al Norte, al Norte los fríos,
las escarchas y las nieves!
Por donde vienen fascistas,
negras cruces en el vientre,
desatad los vendavales,
que venga el crujir de dientes;
arrancadles las guerreras,
las sotanas y bonetes,
que vuestras noches de frío
a ellos les lleve la muerte.
¡Viento colado del puerto
por Marichiva y Minguete,
cortadles como cuchillos,
en rebanadas calientes,

you still had your aeroplane,
and you never wavered for a moment
in using your death to demolish
that traitorous invader.
If you were left lifeless,
may your memory live forever!

MANUEL ALTOLAGUIRRE

The Cold in the Sierra

Malagosto, severe summit,
to be still is to your advantage.
Reventón, let your inaccessible reaches
be those of warm lands.
Hills of icy winds,
be now those of green gardens,
so the people's soldiers
won't freeze along the front.
Summits of frozen breezes,
hold fast with your snows awhile.
Storm clouds of autumns,
sad cold of September,
don't wound the militiamen
who spend the night at the front.
Stay to the north, to the north,
cold, frost and the snows!
Wherever the fascists come from,
black crosses upon their bellies,
let loose with your gales,
may the chattering of teeth come;
rip the tunics off of them,
and their soutanes and birettas,
may death bring them
those cold nights of yours.
Cold, howling winds in the passes
of Marichiva and Minguete,
cut them like knives,
cut their donkey ears

las orejas de borricos,
los sonrosados mofletes,
la baja mirada hipócrita
y la intención de serpiente!
¡Respetad los milicianos,
tristes fríos de septiembre:
España lucha con ellos,
lo mejor que España tiene!

JOSE HERRERA PETERE

into slices so hot,
and their blushing chubby cheeks,
their lowered, hypocritical gaze,
their snake-like intentions!
Respect the militiamen,
sad cold of September:
for with them Spain struggles on,
they're the best that Spain has!

JOSE HERRERA PETERE

ROMANCES BURLESCOS

El Mulo Mola

El hijo de la gran Mula
por Mola vino a las malas.
Como no tuvo soldados,
los hizo con las sotanas.
De lejos, el traidor Franco
sólo promesas le manda,
y tomándolo por Mulo
le anuncia tropas mulatas.
Ya están pidiendo madrinas
las tropas de las mejalas.
La Media Luna ya tiene
protección de las beatas.
¡Cómo curan sus heridas,
cómo el moro les regala
sangrientos ramos de flores
llenos de orejas cortadas!
En mulas van hacia Mola
pidiendo a gritos la paga.
Mola los muele con **marcos**,
ya caducos, de Alemania.
¡Fiero moro, te engañaron,
te van a engañar, te engañan!
De todas partes por radio
llegan las voces cascadas
de generales borrachos
diciendo botaratadas.
Mientras que contra los cuentos
que los fascistas levantan,
las hoces y los martillos
chocan sus verdades claras.
Las Milicias van cantando
su alegría en la batalla,
victoriosas de la muerte
que acecha a sus milicianas;
siempre poniendo los ojos
en donde ponen las balas.

BURLESQUE ROMANCES

The Mule Mola[3]

That son of the great She-Mule
through Mola he came to do mischief.
As he didn't have any soldiers,
he made them up out of soutanes.
From far away the traitor Franco
sends him only promises
and taking him for a Mule
proclaims the coming of mulatto troops.
Now they're asking for war mothers,
these troops from the mehallas.
The Crescent now has the protection
of those zealously pious women.
And how they cure their wounds,
and how the Moor gives them
bloodied bunches of flowers
filled with severed ears!
On mules they go towards Mola
shouting for their pay.
Mola strings them along with *marks*,
those from Germany, long out of use.
Fierce Moor, they tricked you,
are going to trick you, are tricking you!
And from all parts
come the cracking voices
of drunken generals
spouting drivel over the radio.
Meanwhile, against these tales
which the fascists raise,
hammers and sickles smash
their clear truths.
And in battle our Militias
go about singing of their joy,
victorious over the death that lies
in ambush for their militiawomen;
always putting their bullets
where they've put their eyes.

Asoma la luz del día
enfrente de Guadarrama,
ensangrentando de albores
las luces de la esperanza.
Al otro lado del monte
está la muerte de España.

JOSE BERGAMIN

Radio Sevilla

¡Atención! Radio Sevilla.
Queipo de Llano es quien ladra,
quien muge, quien gargajea,
quien rebuzna a cuatro patas.
¡Radio Sevilla!—Señores:
aquí un salvador de España.
¡Viva el vino, viva el vómito!
Esta noche tomo Málaga;
el lunes, tomé Jerez;
martes, Montilla y Cazalla;
miércoles, Chinchón, y el jueves,
borracho y por la mañana,
todas las caballerizas
de Madrid, todas las cuadras,
mullendo los cagajones,
me darán su blanda cama.
¡Oh, qué delicia dormir
teniendo por almohada,
y al alcance del hocico
dos pesebreras de alfalfa!
¡Qué honor ir al herradero
del ronzal! ¡Qué insigne gracia
recibir en mis pezuñas,
clavadas con alcayatas,
las herraduras que Franco
ganó por arrojo en Africa!
Ya se me atiranta el lomo,
ya se me empinan las ancas,

The light of day breaks out
there in front of the Guadarrama,
bloodstaining the lights of hope
with the light of dawn.
On the other side of the hills
is the death of Spain.

JOSE BERGAMIN

Radio Sevilla[4]

Attention! Radio Sevilla,
Queipo de Llano is the one barking,
who roars, who coughs up phlegm,
who is braying on all fours.
Radio Sevilla! *"Señores:*
here is a savior of Spain.
Long live wine, long live vomit!
Tonight I'll have Málaga;[5]
Monday I had Jerez;
Tuesday, Montilla and Cazalla;
Wednesday, Chinchón; and Thursday,
drunk and in the morning,
all the coach houses of Madrid,
all the stables
—fluffing up the horseshit—
will offer me their soft bed.
Oh, what a delight to sleep,
having for a pillow
and within easy reach of my snout
two whole stalls of alfalfa!
What an honor to go to the blacksmith
in a bridle! What an eminent favor
to receive on my hooves,
driven in with spikes,
the horseshoes that Franco
won for daring in Africa!
Already my back is tightening,
now my haunches are rearing up,

ya las orejas me crecen,
ya los dientes se me alargan,
la cincha me viene corta,
las riendas se me desmandan,
galopo, galopo... al paso.
Estaré en Madrid mañana.
Que los colegios se cierren,
que las tabernas se abran.
Nada de Universidades,
de Institutos, nada, nada.
Que el vino corra al encuentro
de un libertador de España.
—¡Atención! Radio Sevilla.
El general de esta plaza,
tonto berrendo en idiota,
Queipo de Llano, se calla.

RAFAEL ALBERTI

now my ears are growing on me,
now my teeth are lengthening,
the cinch is becoming small,
my reins break me loose,
I gallop and gallop...not pausing.
Tomorrow I'll be in Madrid.
Let the schools close,
let the taverns open.
And not a word about Universities,
about High Schools, nothing, nothing.
Let the wine flow on meeting up
with a true liberator of Spain."
"Attention! Radio Sevilla.
The general of this post,
Queipo de Llano, stupidly shrieking
like an idiot, has shut up."

RAFAEL ALBERTI

ROMANCES DE MOROS

El Moro Fugado

Mañana de Peguerinos,
con El Escorial al fondo.
Ladra la ametralladora.
Suben, lo mismo que troncos,
entre los troncos, los hombres:
son españoles y moros.
Abajo San Rafael
los protege. Suben, trovos,
regulares de Larache
mandados contra nosotros
por oficiales del crimen
que a sí se dicen católicos.
Busta Ben Alí Mohamed,
barba negra, negros ojos,
negro, de sus avanzadas
se desprende sigiloso.
Y arrastrándose en la hierba
dice, alzándose de pronto,
el puño en alto, tranquilo,
ante los fusiles solo:
—Yo estar rojo, camaradas.
No tiréis, que yo estar rojo.

ANTONIO GARCIA LUQUE
(RAFAEL ALBERTI)

ROMANCES OF MOORS

The Runaway Moor

A Peguerinos morning,
with El Escorial in the background.
The machine gun is barking away.
Men, just like tree trunks,
among the tree trunks, are climbing:
they are Spaniards and Moors.
Down below, San Rafael protects them.
Regulares from Larache,
fierce-looking, are climbing,
ordered against us
by the officers of this crime
who claim they are Catholics.
Busta Ben Ali Mohamed,
black beard, eyes black,
black, from their scouting detail
he secretly breaks away.
And crawling along in the grass
he says, jumping up suddenly,
his fist raised high, calm,
alone in front of the guns:
"I *is* a Red, comrades,
don't shoot, I *is* a Red."

ANTONIO GARCIA LUQUE
(RAFAEL ALBERTI)

ROMANCES LIRICOS

Llegada

A Federico García Lorca

Alamedas de mi sangre.
¡Alto dolor de olmos negros!
¿Qué nuevos vientos lleváis?
¿Qué murmuran vuestros ecos?
¿Qué apretáis en mi garganta
que siento el tallo del hielo
aún más frío que la muerte
estrangular mi deseo?
¿Qué agudo clamor de angustia
rueda corazón adentro
golpe a golpe, retumbando
como campana de duelo,
ahuecándome las venas,
turbando mi pensamiento,
prendiendo mis libres ojos,
segando mi vista al viento!
¿Qué rumor llevan tus hojas
que todo mi cuerpo yerto
bajo sus dolientes ramas
ni duerme ni está despierto,
ni vivo ni muerto atiende
a la voz de ningún dueño,
que va, como un río sin agua,
andando en pie por un sueño?
Con cinco llamas agudas
clavadas sobre su pecho,
sin pensamiento y sin sombra,
vaga con temblor de espectro
por ciudades y jardines,
al mar libre y en los puertos,
triste pájaro sin alas
acribillado a luceros.
Alamedas de mi sangre,
decid, ¿qué amargo secreto

LYRICAL ROMANCES

Arrival

To Federico García Lorca

Poplar groves of my blood.
High sorrow of black elm trees!
What new winds are you wearing?
What are your echoes murmuring?
What are you tightening in my throat
so that I feel this stem of ice,
even colder than death,
strangling my desire?
What a strident clamor of anguish
that spins beat by beat
within my heart, resounding
like bells of mourning,
hollowing out my veins,
troubling my thoughts,
setting my free eyes ablaze,
sowing my vision to the wind!
What rumor do your leaves bear
so that my whole stiff body
beneath its pained branches
neither sleeps nor is awake,
neither dead nor alive pays heed
to the voice of any master,
that travels firmly through
a dream like a waterless river?
With five sharp flames
driven into its breast,
without thought or shadow,
this sad and wingless bird
riddled with stars
wanders trembling like a ghost
through cities and gardens,
out to the free seas and in ports.
Poplar groves of my blood,
do tell: what bitter secret

mordió las sanas raíces
que os da vida y movimiento?
Vine de Málaga roja,
de Málaga roja vengo,
vine lleno de banderas
y toda la sangre ardiendo.
Llegué a Madrid perseguido
de enemigos pensamientos,
aún con rumores de lucha
y con zumbidos de truenos;
más de mil brazos traía
alrededor de mi cuerpo,
saludando mi alegría,
desatando mi silencio.
Amigos, vengo de Málaga,
aún me huele a sal el sueño,
me huele a pescado y gloria,
a espuma y a sol de fuego.
Mucho que contaros traigo,
mucho que contar, y bueno.
Amigos, os hallé a todos,
alegres, en vuestros puestos.
¿En dónde está Federico?
A él sólo de menos echo,
y a él tengo más que contarle,
mucho que contarle tengo.
¿En dónde está Federico?
Sólo responde el silencio:
un temor se va agrandando,
temor que encoge los pechos.
De noche los olivares
alzan los brazos gimiendo.
La luna lo anda buscando,
rodando, lenta, en el cielo.
La sangre de los gitanos
lo llama abierta en el suelo;
más gritos lleva la sombra
que estrellas el firmamento.
Las madrugadas preguntan
por él temblando de miedo.
¡Qué gran tumba esta distancia
que calla su hondo misterio!
Vengo de Málaga roja,

gnawed upon those healthy roots
that gave you life and movement?
I came from red Málaga,
from red Málaga I've come,
I came loaded down with flags
and all my blood aflame.
I arrived in Madrid
pursued by hostile thoughts,
still with rumblings of battle
and the whistling of barrages;
about my body I brought
more than a thousand arms,
greeting everyone with my joy,
bursting out of my silence.
Friends, I've come from Málaga,
my dream still smells of salt,
of fish and of glory,
of foam and of fiery sun.
Many things to tell you I've brought,
many things, and all good.
Friends, I found you joyous
and at your posts.
But, where is Federico?
For it's he alone I miss,
and I've much more to tell him,
much to tell him have I.
What's become of Federico?
Only the silence responds:
a fear begins to grow in me,
fear that freezes the soul.
At night the olive groves
raise their limbs and wail.
The moon goes searching for him,
spinning slowly in the sky.
The Gypsies' blood, open
upon the ground, calls to him;
more screams are carried by the shadows
than stars by the firmament.
Trembling with fright
the dawns ask about him.
What a great tomb is this distance
that silences its profound mystery!
I've come from red Málaga,

31

de Málaga roja vengo;
levántate, Federico,
álzate en pie sobre el viento,
mira que llego del mar,
mucho que contarte tengo:
Málaga tiene otras playas
y grandes peces de acero
con mil ojos vigilantes
defienden firmes su puerto.
¿En dónde estás, Federico?
Yo este rumor no lo creo.
¡Cómo me duelen las balas
que hoy circundan tu recuerdo!
Desde Málaga a Granada,
rojos pañuelos al cuello,
gitanos y pescadores
van con anillos de hierro:
sortijas que envía la muerte
a tus negros carceleros.
Aguárdame, Federico,
mucho que contarte espero.
Entre Málaga y Granada,
una barrera de fuego.

EMILIO PRADOS

Viento del Pueblo

Sentado sobre los muertos
que se han callado en dos meses,
beso zapatos vacíos
y empuño rabiosamente
la mano del corazón
y el alma que lo mantiene.
Que mi voz suba a los montes
y baje a la tierra y truene,
eso pide mi garganta
desde ahora y desde siempre.
Acércate a mi clamor,

from red Málaga I've come;
arise Federico,
rise to your feet upon the wind
and see that I've come from the sea,
much to tell you have I:
Málaga has different beaches,
and large steel fish
with a thousand vigilant eyes
steadfastly defending its port.
What's become of you, Federico?
This rumor I do not believe.
How I'm wounded by the bullets
that today surround your memory!
From Málaga to Granada,
Gypsies and fishermen,
red scarves around the neck,
go about with rings of iron:
rings that send death
to your black jailers.
Await me, Federico,
there's much I hope to tell you.
Between Málaga and Granada,
a barrier of fire.

EMILIO PRADOS

Winds of the People

Sitting on top of the dead
who've fallen silent in two months,
I kiss empty shoes
and grasp furiously
at the heart's hand
and the soul that supports it.
Let my voice rise to the mountains
and descend to earth and thunder,
that is what my throat asks,
from now on and always.
Draw close to my clamor,

pueblo de mi misma leche,
árbol que con tus raíces
encarcelado me tienes,
que aquí estoy yo para amarte
y estoy para defenderte
con la sangre y con la boca
como dos fusiles fieles.
Si yo salí de la tierra,
si yo he nacido de un vientre
desdichado y con pobreza,
no fué sino para hacerme
ruiseñor de las desdichas,
eco de la mala suerte,
y cantar y repitir
a quien escucharme debe
cuanto a penas, cuanto a pobres,
cuanto a tierra se refiere.
Ayer amaneció el pueblo
desnudo y sin qué ponerse,
hambriento y sin qué comer,
y el día de hoy amanece
justamente aborrascado
y sangriento justamente.
En su mano los fusiles
leones quieren volverse
para acabar con las fieras
que lo han sido tantas veces.
Aunque te falten las armas,
pueblo de cien mil poderes,
no desfallezcan tus huesos,
castiga a quien te malhiere
mientras que te queden puños,
uñas, saliva, y te queden
corazón, entrañas, tripas,
cosas de varón y dientes.
Bravo como el viento bravo,
leve como el aire leve,
asesina al que asesina,
aborrece al que aborrece
la paz de tu corazón
y el vientre de tus mujeres.
No te hieran por la espalda,
vive cara a cara y muere

people of my very own milk,
tree that keeps me imprisoned
amongst your roots,
for I am here to love you
and here to defend you
with my blood and my mouth
that are like two faithful guns.
If I emerged from the earth,
if I was born of a wretched
and impoverished womb,
it was but to make myself
a nightingale of misfortunes,
an echo of bad luck,
and to sing and sing again,
for those who ought to hear me,
about everything regarding suffering,
the poor, regarding the land.
Yesterday the people awoke
naked and with nothing to wear,
hungry and with nothing to eat,
and today is dawning
justifiably stormy
and bleeding in fact.
In their hands, guns
—lions they wish to become—
to finish off those wild beasts
who've been just that so many times.
Although you lack the weapons,
people of a hundred thousand powers,
don't let your bones weaken,
punish those who badly wound you,
while you still have fists,
nails, spit, and you still have
your heart, entrails, guts,
a man's parts and teeth.
Brave as the brave wind,
light as a light breeze,
murder the one who murders,
detest the one who detests
the peace within your heart
and the wombs of your women.
Let them not wound you from behind,
live always face to face and die

con el pecho ante las balas,
ancho como las paredes.
Canto con la voz de luto,
pueblo de mí, por tus héroes;
tus ansias como las mías,
tus desventuras que tienen
del mismo metal el llanto,
las penas del mismo temple
y de la misma madera
tu pensamiento y mi frente,
tu corazón y mi sangre,
tu dolor y mis laureles.
Antemuro de la nada
esta vida me parece.
Aquí estoy para vivir
mientras el alma me suene,
y aquí estoy para morir,
cuando la hora me llegue,
en los veneros del pueblo
desde ahora y desde siempre.
Varios tragos es la vida
y un solo trago es la muerte.

MIGUEL HERNANDEZ

Ciudad Sitiada

Entre cañones me miro,
entre cañones me muevo:
Castillos de mi razón
y fronteras de mi sueño,
¿dónde comienza mi entraña
y dónde termina el viento?
No tengo pulso en mis venas,
sino zumbidos de trueno,
torbellinos que me arrastran
por las selvas de mis nervios:
multitudes que me empujan,
ojos que queman mi fuego,

with your chest, broad like
a wall, facing the bullets.
I sing with grief-filled voice,
my people, for your heroes;
your anguish the same as mine,
your misfortunes, whose weeping
is that of the same metal,
your sorrows of the same temper;
and of the same timber:
your thoughts and my brow,
your heart and my blood,
your pain and my laurels.
Ramparts of nothingness
this life seems to me.
I am here to live
while the soul resounds,
and I am here to die
when that time does come,
from now on and always
amid the sources of my people.
Several drafts is life,
and death but one draft.

MIGUEL HERNANDEZ

Besieged City

Among cannons I see myself,
among cannons I move about:
Castles of my reason
and frontiers of my dream,
where does my essence begin
and where does the wind end?
I don't have a pulse in my veins,
rather the whistling of barrages,
whirlwinds dragging me along
through the jungles of my nerves:
multitudes shoving me along,
eyes burning up my fire,

bocanadas de victoria,
himnos de sangre y acero,
pájaros que me combaten
y alzan mi frente a su cielo
y ardiendo dejan las nubes
y tembloroso mi suelo.
¡Allá van! Pesadas moles
cruzan mis venas de hierro;
toda mi firmeza aguarda
parapetada en mis huesos.
Compañeros del presente,
fantasmas de mi recuerdo,
esperanzas de mis manos
y nostalgias de mis juegos:
¡Todos en pie, a defenderse!
Que está mi vida en asedio,
que está la verdad sitiada,
amenazada en su pecho.
¡Pronto en pie, las barricadas,
que el corazón está ardiendo!
No han de llegar a apagarlo
negors disparos de hielo.
¡Pronto, deprisa, mi sangre,
arremolíname entero!
Levanta todas mis armas:
mira que aguarda en el centro,
temblando, un turbión de llamas
que ya no cabe en mi cerco.
¡Pronto, a las armas mi sangre,
que ya me rebosa el fuego!
Quien se atreva a amenazarme
tizón se le hará su sueño.
¡Ay, ciudad, ciudad sitiada,
ciudad de mi propio pecho,
si te pisa el enemigo
antes he de verme muerto!
Castillos de mi razón
y fronteras de mi sueño,
mi ciudad está sitiada,
entre cañones me muevo.
¿Dónde comienzas, Madrid,
o es Madrid, que eres mi cuerpo?

EMILIO PRADOS

sudden gusts of victory,
hymns of blood and steel,
birds that do battle with me
and lift my brow to their sky
and leave the clouds ablaze
and my earth trembling.
There they go! Heavy masses
cross over my iron veins;
all my resolve awaits
entrenched in my bones.
Present companions,
ghosts from my memory,
the hopes of my hands
and nostalgia of childhood play:
Rise up, defend yourselves!
My life is under siege,
truth is being besieged,
threatened in its breast.
Rise up quickly, barricades,
for my heart is aflame!
Those black discharges of ice
mustn't manage to put it out.
Quick, fast, blood of mine,
whirl completely through me!
Raise up all my weapons:
look what awaits in the center,
trembling: a shower of flames
that no longer fits in my ambit.
Quick, to your arms, my blood,
for now the fire overflows me!
Whoever dares threaten me,
cinders will be his dream.
Oh, city, besieged city,
city of my own heart,
if the enemy sets foot in you,
I'll see myself dead first!
Castles of my reason
and frontiers of my dream,
my city is being besieged,
among cannons I move about.
Where do you begin, Madrid,
or is it, Madrid, you're my body?

EMILIO PRADOS

39

Viento del Pueblo

Vientos del pueblo me llevan,
vientos del pueblo me arrastran,
me esparcen el corazón
y me avientan la garganta.
Los bueyes doblan la frente,
impotentemente mansa,
delante de los castigos;
los leones la levantan
y al mismo tiempo castigan
con su clamorosa zarpa.
No soy de un pueblo de bueyes,
que soy de un pueblo que embargan
yacimientos de leones,
desfiladeros de águilas
y cordilleras de toros
con el orgullo en el asta.
Nunca medraron los bueyes
en los páramos de España.
¿Quién habló de echar un yugo
sobre el cuello de esta raza?
¿Quién ha puesto al huracán
jamás ni yugos ni tarbas,
ni quién al rayo retuvo
prisonero en una jaula?
Asturianos de braveza,
vascos de piedra blindada,
valencianos de alegría
y castellanos de alma,
labrados como la tierra
y airosos como las alas;
andaluces de relámpagos,
nacidos entre guitarras
y forjados en los yunques
torrenciales de las lágrimas;
extremeños de centeno,
gallegos de lluvia y calma,
catalanes de firmeza,

Winds of the People

Winds of the people carry me away,
winds of the people drag me along,
scattering my heart
and inflating my throat.
Oxen bow their head,
impotently tame,
in the face of punishments;
lions raise theirs
and at the same time punish
with their clamorous claw.
I'm not from a nation of oxen,
I'm from a people who impede
the nocturnal grazing of lions,
the narrow passes of the eagle
and the mountain ranges of bulls
with pride in the horn.
Never did oxen flourish
on the Spanish wastelands.
Whoever spoke of throwing a yoke
over the neck of this race?
Who has ever put yokes
or hobbles on a hurricane,
or kept a flash of lightning
prisoner in a cage?
Asturians of fierceness,
Basques of armored stone,
Valencians of joy
and Castilians of soul,
worked like the soil
and as graceful as wings;
Andalusians of lightning,
born amongst guitars
and forged upon torrential
anvils of tears;
Estremadurans of rye,
Galicians of rain and calm,
Catalans of resolve,

aragoneses de casta,
murcianos de dinamita
frutalmente propagada,
leoneses, navarros, dueños
del hambre, el sudor y el hacha,
reyes de la minería,
señores de la labranza,
hombres que entre las raíces,
como raíces gallardas,
vais de la vida a la muerte,
vais de la nada a la nada:
yugos os quieren poner
gentes de la hierba mala,
yugos que habéis de dejar
rotos sobre sus espaldas.
Crepúsculo de los bueyes
está despuntando el alba.
Los bueyes mueren vestidos
de humildad y olor de cuadra,
las águilas, los leones
y los toros de arrogancia,
y detrás de ellos, el cielo
ni se enturbia ni se acaba.
La agonía de los bueyes
tiene pequeña la cara,
la del animal varón
toda la creación agranda.
Si me muero, que me muera
con la cabeza muy alta.
Muerto y viente veces muerto,
la boca contra la grama,
tendré apretados los dientes
y decidida la barba.
Cantando espero a la muerte,
que hay ruiseñores que cantan
encima de los fusiles
y en medio de las batallas.

MIGUEL HERNANDEZ

Aragonese of pure caste,
Murcians of dynamite
fruitfully propagated,
Leonese, Navarrese, masters
of hunger, sweat and the axe,
kings of mining,
lords of the tilled soil,
men who amongst the roots,
like gallant roots,
you go from life to death,
from nothingness to nothingness:
people of the bad seed
wish to put yokes on you,
yokes that you must leave
broken across their backs.
Twilight of the oxen,
our dawn is breaking.
Oxen die clad in humility
and the smell of the stable;
eagles, lions
and bulls, in arrogance;
and behind them, the sky
neither darkens nor ends.
The death throes of oxen
have a mean countenance,
those of the masculine animal
enlarge all of creation.
If I must die, let me die
with my head held high.
Dead and twenty times dead,
my mouth against the grama grass,
I'll have my teeth clenched
and my beard decided.
Singing I await death,
for there are nightingales that sing
above the guns
and in the midst of battles.

MIGUEL HERNANDEZ

Nunca Jamás Será Esclava

España, la laboriosa,
jamás derramó sus lágrimas
ante Felipe segundo
ni ante el cruel Torquemada.
España, la roja y libre,
nunca jamás será esclava.
España, la laboriosa,
nunca sabrá verter lágrimas
ante los Francos y Molas,
Queipos de Llanos y Arandas.
Hacer frente sólo sabe
en el campo de batalla.
España, la laboriosa,
nunca sabrá verter lágrimas
ante las mil injusticias
que el vil fascismo le causa.
España, la roja y libre,
nunca jamás será esclava.
España, la laboriosa,
nunca sabrá verter lágrimas
ni jamás se humillará
ante la vil clerigalla,
ni ante el criminal fascismo,
ni ante obispos, ni ante el Papa.
España, la laboriosa,
sabe bien librar su causa;
ofrenda su roja sangre
entre cerros y montañas
por una España feliz,
libre, culta y democrática.
España, la roja y libre,
nunca jamás será esclava.

V. DE BODA (Miliciano del batallón "E. Thaelmann")

Never Ever Will She Be a Slave

Spain, the hard working,
never spilled her tears
before Felipe the Second,
nor before the cruel Torquemada.
Spain, the Red and the free,
never ever will she be a slave.
Spain, the hard working,
never will she know how to shed tears
before these Francos and Molas,
Quiepos de Llanos and Arandas.
She knows only how to confront them
on the field of battle.
Spain, the hard working,
never will she know how to shed tears
before the thousands of injustices
that this vile fascism causes her.
Spain, the Red and the free,
never ever will she be a slave.
Spain, the hard working,
never will she know how to shed tears,
nor ever humble herself before
that vile cabal of the cloth,
nor before that criminal fascism,
nor before bishops, nor before the Pope.
Spain, the hard working,
knows how to preserve her cause;
she offers up her red blood
among the hills and mountains
for a happy, free,
cultured and democratic Spain.
Spain, the Red and the free,
never ever will she be a slave.

V. DE BODA *(Militiaman of the "E. Thaelmann" battalion)*

ROMANCES DE LA DEFENSA DE MADRID

Defensa de Madrid, Defensa de Cataluña

I

Madrid, corazón de España,
late con pulsos de fiebre.
Si ayer la sangre le hervía,
hoy con más calor le hierve.
Ya nunca podrá dormirse,
porque si Madrid se duerme,
querrá despertarse un día
y el alba no vendrá a verle.
No olvides, Madrid, la guerra;
jamás olvides que enfrente
los ojos del enemigo
te echan miradas de muerte.
Rodan por tu cielo halcones
que precipitarse quieren
sobre tus rojos tejados,
tus calles, tu brava gente.
Madrid: que nunca se diga,
nunca se publique o piense
que en el corazón de España
la sangre se volvió nieve.
Fuentes de valor y hombría
las guardas tú donde siempre.
Atroces ríos de asombro
han de correr de esas fuentes.
Que cada barrio, a su hora,
si esa mal hora viniere
—hora que no vendrá—sea
más que la plaza más fuerte.
Los hombres, como castillos;
igual que almenas, sus frentes,
grandes murallas sus brazos,

ROMANCES OF THE DEFENSE OF MADRID

Defense of Madrid, Defense of Catalonia

I

Madrid, the heart of Spain,
beats with feverish pulses.
If yesterday its blood was boiling,
today it is boiling even hotter.
Now Madrid won't be able to sleep,
for if Madrid does sleep,
one day it will want to awake
and the dawn won't come to visit.
Never forget the war, Madrid;
never once forget that the eyes
of the enemy there in front are
casting deadly gazes at you.
Patrolling your skies are falcons
that want to hurl themselves
down upon your red tiled roofs,
your streets, your brave people.
Madrid: may it never be said,
never be proclaimed or thought
that here in the heart of Spain
blood turns into snow.
Springs of valor and manliness you keep
in the same place as always.
Atrocious rivers of fright
must flow from those springs.
Let each neighborhood, when the time comes,
if that evil time does come
—time that will never come—be
stronger than the strongest plaza.
The men, like castles;
just like battlements, their brows;
great walls, their arms;

47

puertas que nadie penetre.
Quien al corazón de España
quiera asomarse, que llegue.
¡Pronto! Madrid está lejos.
Madrid sabe defenderse
con uñas, con pies, con codos,
con empujones, con dientes,
panza arriba, arisco, recto,
duro, al pie del agua verde
del Tajo, en Navalperal,
en Sigüenza, en donde suenen
balas y balas que busquen
helar su sangre caliente.
Madrid, corazón de España,
que es de tierra, dentro tiene,
si se le escarba, un gran hoyo,
profundo, grande, imponente,
como un barranco que aguarda...
Sólo en él cabe la muerte.

II

¡Catalanes! Cataluña,
vuestra hermosa madre tierra,
tan de vuestros corazones
como tan hermana nuestra,
con un costado en el mar
y entre montes la cabeza,
soñado en sus libertades
sus hijos manda a la guerra.
Camino de Zaragoza
frente a los muros de Huesca,
por los llanos de Toledo,
por toda España entera,
va la sangre catalana
sonando al son de su lengua.
Mas para seguir sonando
el son de lo que tú sueñas,
no te olivdes, Cataluña,
que a Madrid, lejos, lo acechan
miradas del enemigo,
que darles muerte quisieran.
Muerto Madrid, catalanes,

gates that no one can penetrate.
Whoever wishes to gaze out upon
the heart of Spain, let him come.
But soon! For Madrid is far away.
Madrid knows how to defend itself
with nails, with feet, with elbows,
by shoving and using its teeth,
the gut in, surly, standing straight,
hard, there along the banks
of the Tajo's green waters,
at Navalperal, at Sigüenza,
wherever bullets ring out and where
bullets seek to freeze its hot blood.
Madrid, the heart of Spain,
one made of earth, has within it,
if you scratch the surface, a great pit,
deep, large, imposing,
like some gorge that is awaiting...
And only death will fit into it.

II

Catalans! Catalonia,
your beautiful motherland,
so close to your hearts
and such a sister to us,
with her side in the sea
and her head among the mountains,
dreaming about her freedoms,
she sends her sons off to war.
On the road to Zaragoza
facing the walls of Huesca,
through the plains of Toledo,
over the whole length of Spain,
flows this Catalonian blood,
sounding to the sound of its tongue.
But to keep on sounding the sound
of what you are dreaming about,
never once forget, Catalonia,
that those gazes of the enemy
are lying in ambush, wanting
to put Madrid, far away, to death.
Once Madrid is dead, Catalans—

¡qué invasión, qué turba negra,
qué prostituída, oscura,
qué cruel y extraña leva
de gentes intentarían
forzar tus gallardas puertas!
Si ahora Madrid es el centro,
corazón de la pelea,
parados sus firmes pulsos,
tú serías la cabeza,
el cuello más codiciado,
la más codiciada prenda.
¡Qué festín de generales
borrachos, ante una mesa
donde por blancos manteles
se usaran ropas sangrientas!
¡Nunca, bravos catalanes!
Jamás vuestra independencia
debe servirse en banquetes
a monstruos de tal ralea.
La libertad catalana,
¡sabedlo!, en Madrid se juega:
fábricas, ciudades, campos,
montes, toda la riqueza
de vuestro país, y el mar
que lo ilumina y le entrega
barcos que al tocar las costas
se vuelven de plata nueva.
¡Pueblo catalán, vigila!
¡Pueblo catalán, alerta!
Con el corazón de España,
sólo corazón de tierra,
catalanes, yo os saludo:
¡Viva vuestra independencia!

RAFAEL ALBERTI

what an invasion, what a black mob,
what a prostituted, obscure…
what a cruel and strange rabble
of conscripts who would try to
force open your gallant gates!
If Madrid is now the center,
the heart of the struggle,
its firm heartbeats stopped,
then you would be its head,
the neck most coveted,
the most coveted jewel.
What a fest for drunken generals
seated before a table where,
for the white tablecloths,
they'd use bloodied clothing!
Never, brave Catalans!
Never must your independence
be served up at banquets
to monsters of such a breed.
This Catalonian freedom—
understand!—is at stake in Madrid:
factories, cities, fields, mountains,
all the wealth of your country,
and the sea which illuminates it
and to it delivers boats that,
upon touching its coasts,
become of new silver.
People of Catalonia, take care!
People of Catalonia, watch out!
With the heart of Spain,
that is only a heart of earth,
I hail you, Catalans:
Long live your independence!

RAFAEL ALBERTI

¡Alerta, los Madrileños!

I

Pueblo de Madrid valiente,
pueblo de paz y trabajo,
defiéndete contra aquellas
fieras que te están cercando;
ellas tienen por oficio
la destrucción y el estrago,
ellos hacen de la guerra
un arte para tu daño.
Si por amor a la paz
estuvimos desarmados,
por amor a la justicia
ahora el fusil empuñamos.
Demuéstrale al enemigo
que no quieres ser esclavo;
más vale morir de pie
que vivir arrodillados;
cadenas, las que formemos
unidos por nuestros brazos,
unión que nunca se rompa,
vínculo firme de hermanos.
Muros de sacos terreros,
surcos hondos, no de arados
sí con picos y con palas,
con corazones sembrados,
semilla roja seremos
en las trincheras del campo.
Cuando brote la victoria,
con sus palmas y sus ramos,
el mundo verá en nosotros
su más brillante pasado;
seamos la aurora, la fuente,
demos los primeros pasos
del porvenir que en Europa
merece el proletariado.

Attention, People of Madrid!

I

People of valiant Madrid,
people of work and peace,
defend against those wild beasts
that are laying siege to you;
they're making a vocation
out of havoc and destruction,
to harm you they're making
an art out of war.
If out of love for peace
we were unarmed,
for love of justice
we now take up the gun.
Demonstrate to the enemy
you don't wish to be a slave;
it's better to die standing
than to live on one's knees;
chains, the ones we form
by linking our arms,
a union that never breaks,
a firm bond among brothers.
Walls of sandbags,
deep furrows, not of plows
but those of pick and shovel,
and with sown hearts,
red seed we will become
in the trenches of the field.
When victory does blossom,
with its palms and olive branch,
in us the world will see
its most brilliant past;
may we be its dawn, its source,
may we take the first steps
into that future which the
European proletariat deserves.

II

Madrid, capital de Europa,
eje de la lucha obrera,
tantos ojos hoy te miran
que debes estar de fiesta;
vístete con tus hazañas,
adórnate con proezas,
sea tu canto el más valiente,
sean tus luces las más bellas;
cuando una ciudad gloriosa
ante el mundo así se eleva,
debe cuidar su atavío,
debe mostrar que en sus venas
tiene sangre que hasta el rostro
no subirá con vergüenza,
sí con la fiebre que da
el vigor en la contienda.
Madrid, te muerden las faldas
canes de mala ralea,
vuelan cuervos que vomitan
sucia metralla extranjera.
Lucha alegre, lucha, vence,
envuélvete en tu bandera.
Te están mirando, te miran,
que no te olviden con pena.

MANUEL ALTOLAGUIRRE

II

Madrid, capital of Europe,
hub of the workers struggle,
today so many eyes are upon you
that you should be celebrating;
dress yourself in your feats,
adorn yourself with exploits,
may your song be the most valiant,
may your lights be the most lovely;
when a glorious city is held up
in such a way before the world,
it should look after its dress,
it should show that the blood
which runs through its veins
won't redden its face with shame,
but rather with the fever
that gives it vigor in combat.
Madrid, canines of an evil breed
are nipping at your shirttails,
and crows are flying about
vomiting dirty foreign shrapnel.
Joyous struggle, struggle, conquer,
wrap yourself in your flag;
eyes are upon you, observing you;
may they never ruefully forget you.

MANUEL ALTOLAGUIRRE

EDICIONES ESPAÑOLAS

MADRID - VALENCIA 1937

POETAS
EN LA ESPAÑA
LEAL

Antonio Machado, Rafael Alberti, Manuel Altolaguirre, Luis Cernuda, Juan Gil-Albert, Miguel Hernández, León-Felipe, José Moreno Villa, Emilio Prados, Arturo Serrano Plaja y Lorenzo Varela.

Poets in Loyalist Spain

Once the euphoria of the first months of civil war had cooled, another type of war poetry began to appear, one that was introspective, subjective, even elitist, but always touched by the events that the poets and the Spanish people were living through. Apart from the psychological letdown, the poet found that he needed to go beyond the limits of the romance form, even if it meant sacrificing the immediate goals of agitation and propaganda in order to search for transcendent values. Although romances were written throughout the Spanish Civil War, there was a growing awareness that if poetry was to be an arm against injustice, then it must fight on all fronts.

In *Poets in Loyalist Spain,* published to commemorate the Second International Congress of Anti-fascist Writers, we have a diversity of style ranging from the stark, almost un-poetic verse of Moreno Villa—or the simple, pure line of Manuel Altolaguirre—to the *culteranismo* or Gongorism of Alberti and Cernuda, characterized by an ornate and intricate style, complex syntax, brusque changes of tense and obscurity of meaning. There is also the verse of Miguel Hernández, whose classical style had been tempered by Neruda's and Aleixandre's influence; León Felipe, with his anarchistic, Whitmanesque tones; Prados, whose poetry is touched by that same Andalusian "superrealism" which one finds in Lorca; Antonio Machado's impressive poem dedicated to Lorca's memory, "The Crime Took Place in Granada"; the baroque flights of Serrano Plaja and Gil-Albert; and the youthful laments of Lorenzo Varela.

The Spanish Civil War was barely a year old when *Poets in Loyalist Spain* appeared in July of 1937.

El Crimen fué en Granada

A Federico García Lorca

I

(EL CRIMEN)

Se le vió, caminando entre fusiles
por una calle larga,
salir al campo frío,
aún con estrellas, de la madrugada.
Mataron a Federico
cuando la luz asomaba.
El pelotón de verdugos
no osó mirarle a la cara.
Todos cerraron los ojos;
rezaron: ¡ni Dios te salva!
Muerto cayó Federico
—sangre en la frente y polmo en las entrañas—.
...Que fué en Granada el crimen,
sabed—¡pobre Granada!—, en su Granada!...

II

(EL POETA Y LA MUERTE)

Se le vió caminar solo con Ella,
sin miedo a su guadaña.
—Ya el sol en torre y torre; los martillos
en yunque—, yunque y yunque de las fraguas.
Hablaba Federico,
requebrando a la Muerte. Ella escuchaba.
"Porque ayer en mi verso, compañera,
sonaba el golpe de tus secas palmas,
y diste el hielo a mi cantar, y el filo
a mi tragedia de tu hoz de plata,
te cantaré la carne que no tienes,
los ojos que te faltan,
tus cabellos que el viento sacudía,
los rojos labios donde te besaban...

The Crime Took Place in Granada

To Federico García Lorca

I

(THE CRIME)

He was seen, walking among guns
down a long street,
going out to the cold fields,
still beneath stars before the dawn.
They killed Federico
when light first appeared.
The squad of executioners
dared not look him in the face.
All shut their eyes;
they prayed: "Not even God will save you!"
Dead fell Federico
—blood on his forehead and lead in his guts.
...For in Granada this crime took place,
understand—poor Granada!—in his Granada!...

II

(THE POET AND DEATH)

He was seen walking alone with Her,
unafraid of her reaper.
"The sun already in tower upon tower; hammers
upon anvil," anvil and anvil of the forges.
Federico was speaking,
flirting with death. She listened.
"Because yesterday in my verse, companion,
the blow of your dry palms was sounding,
and you gave ice to my song, and the edge
of your silver sickle to my tragedy.
I'll sing you the flesh you don't have,
the eyes you lack,
the tresses the wind would blow about,
the red lips where they would kiss you...

59

Hoy como ayer, gitana, muerte mía,
qué bien contigo a solas,
por estos aires de Granada, ¡mi Granada!"

III

Se les vió caminar...
                    Labrad, amigos,
de piedra y sueño, en el Alhambra,
un túmulo al poeta,
sobre una fuente donde llore el agua,
y eternamente diga:
el crimen fué en Granada, ¡en su Granada!

ANTONIO MACHADO

Today as yesterday, Gypsy, death of mine,
how good to be alone with you
through these breezes of Granada, my Granada!"

III

They were seen walking...
                    Carve, my friends,
out of stone and dream in the Alhambra,
a tomb for the poet,
above a fountain where water weeps
and eternally says:
the crime took place in Granada, in his Granada!

ANTONIO MACHADO

Capital de la Gloria

Madrid—Otoño

I

Ciudad de los más turbios siniestros provocados,
de la angustia nocturna que ordena hundirse al miedo
en los sótanos lívidos con ojos desvelados,
yo quisiera furiosa, pero impasiblemente
arrancarme de cuajo la voz, pero no puedo,
para pisarte toda tan silenciosamente,
que la sangre tirada
mordiera, sin protesta, mi llanto y mi pisada.

Por tus desnivelados terrenos y arrabales,
ciudad, por tus lluviosas y ateridas afueras
voy las hojas difuntas pisando entre trincheras,
charcos y barrizales.
Los árboles acodan, deprovistos, las ramas
por bardas y tapiales
donde con ojos fijos espían las troneras
un cielo temeroso de explosiones y llamas.
Capital ya madura para los bombardeos,
avenidas de escombros y barrios en ruinas,
corre un escalofrío al pensar tus museos
tras de las barricadas que impiden las esquinas.

Hay casas cuyos muros humildes, levantados
a la escena del aire, representan la escena
del mantel y los lechos todavía ordenados,
el drama silencioso de los trajes vacíos,
sin nadie, en la alacena
que los biseles fríos
de la menguada luna de los pobres roperos
recogen y barajan con los sacos terreros.

Capital of the Glory[1]
Madrid—Autumn

I

City of the most troubling of provoked calamities,
of the nocturnal anguish that orders one to sink into fear
in those livid cellars with watchful eyes,
I would want to furiously, but impassively
pull my voice out by the roots, but I can't,
and tread with such silence completely over you,
so that thrown away blood
would bite into, without protest, my weeping and my footstep.

Through your uneven lands and environs,
city, through your rainy and numbing cold outskirts,
I go along stepping on deceased leaves amid trenches,
puddles and muddy ground.
Trees, stripped clean, rest their branches
over thatched roofs and mud walls
where embrasures would with fixed gaze spy
a frightful sky of explosions and flames.
Capital already ripe for bombings,
avenues of rubble and neighborhoods in ruins,
a shudder runs through one on thinking about your museums
behind the barricades that obstruct the street corners.

There are houses whose walls, raised
upon a scene in the air, stage the scene
of still tidy tablecloth and beds,
the silent drama of empty suits,
with no one in them, in the closet
that the cold chamfers
of the waning moonlight of poor wardrobes
gather up and shuffle together with the sandbags.

Más que nunca mirada,
como ciudad que en tierra reposa al descubierto,
la frente de tu frente se alza tiroteada,
tus costados de áriboles y llanuras, heridos;
pero tu corazón no lo taparán muerto,
aunque montes de escombros le paren sus latidos.

Ciudad, ciudad presente,
guardas en tus entrañas de catástrofe y gloria
el germen más hermoso de tu vida futura.
Bajo la dinamita de tus cielos, crujiente,
se oye el nacer del nuevo hijo de la victoria.
Gritando y a empujones la tierra lo inaugura.

II

¡Palacios, bibliotecas! Estos libros tirados
que la yerba arrasada recibe y no comprende,
estos descoloridos sofás desvencijados
que ya tan sólo el frío los usa y los definde;
estos inesperados
retratos familiares
en donde los varones de la casa, vestidos
los más innecesarios jaeces militares,
nos contemplan, partidos,
sucios, pisoteados,
con ese inexpresable gesto fijo y obscuro
del que al nacer ya lleva contra su espalda el muro
de los ejecutados;
este cuadro, este libro, este furor que ahora
me arranca lo que tienes para mí de elegía
son pedazos de sangre de tu terrible aurora.
Ciudad, quiero ayudarte a dar a luz tu día.

RAFAEL ALBERTI

More than ever observed,
like a city that reposes fully exposed upon the ground,
the face of your front rises up shot full of holes,
your sides of trees and plains, wounded;
but your heart they will never cover up dead,
although mountains of rubble stop its heartbeats.

City, present city,
you hold in your entrails of catastrophe and glory
that most beautiful germ of your future life.
Under the dynamite of your skies, rustling,
the birth of this new child of victory is heard.
Shouting and shoving the earth unveils him.

II

Palaces, libraries! These thrown away books
the scythed grass receives and does not understand,
these discolored, broken-down sofas
that now only the cold uses and defends;
these unexpected
family portraits
in which the males of the house, dressed up in
the most unnecessary military trappings,
contemplate us, torn apart,
dirty, stepped on,
with that inexpressible fixed and obscure expression
of the one who at birth already carries the wall
of the executed on his back;
this painting, this book, this furor, that now
wrench from me what elegy you have for me,
are but bits of blood from your terrible dawn.
City, I wish to help you give birth to your day.

RAFAEL ALBERTI

A Niebla, Mi Perro

Niebla, tú no comprendes: lo cantan tus orejas,
el tobaco inocente, tonto de tu mirada,
los largos resplandores que por el monte dejas,
al saltar, rayo tierno de brizna despeinada.

Mira esos perros turbios, huérfanos, reservados,
que de improviso surgen de las rotas neblinas,
arrastrar en su tímidos pasos desorientados
todo el terror reciente de su casa en ruinas.

A pesar de esos coches fugaces, sin cortejo,
que transportan la muerte en un cajón desnudo;
de ese niño que observa lo mismo que un festejo
la batalla en el aire, que asesinarle pudo;

a pesar del mejor compañero perdido,
de mi más que tristísima familia que no entiende
lo que yo más quisiera que hubiera compendido,
y a pesar del amigo que deserta y nos vende.

Niebla, mi camarada,
aunque tú no lo sabes, nos queda todavía,
en medio de esta heroica pena bombardeada,
la fe, que se alegría, alegría, alegría.

RAFAEL ALBERTI

To Niebla, My Dog

Niebla, you don't understand: your ears sing it,
and the silly, innocent tobacco of your gaze,
and the long radiances that you, tender streak of unkempt wisp,
leave while bounding about in the countryside.

Look at those troubled, orphaned and wary dogs
unexpectedly surging out of the broken mists,
dragging along in the wake of their timid, disoriented steps
all the recent terror of their homes in ruins.

Despite those fleeting, unescorted cars
transporting death around in a naked box,
and the child who watches, like some entertainment,
the battle in the air, that could murder him;

despite losing my best companion,
and my more than bitterly sad family that doesn't grasp
what I would most want them to have understood,
and despite the friend who deserts and sells us out;

Niebla, my comrade,
though you don't know it, we are still,
in the midst of this heroic and bombarded suffering,
left with faith, which is joy, joy, joy.

RAFAEL ALBERTI

Líneas de Fuego

Ultima Muerte

Pido la última muerte de esta guerra
porque quiero mirarme en la corriente
como un dolido cuerpo macerado,
cual árbol que despojan de sus frutos,
al que arrancan sus ramas
y aprovechan el leño de su tronco...

Y si no puedo verme,
si de mí quedan sólo las raíces,
si los pájaros buscan vanamente
el lugar de sus nidos
en las tristes ausencias de mis brazos,
entonces, desde el fondo,
con el silencio de una primavera,
brotarán de la tierra como llanto
insinuaciones de verdor y vida.
Seré esa multitud de adolescentes,
esa corona de laurel que ciñe
el tronco quebrantado por el hacha.
Multiplicada vida da la muerte.
Múltiples son los rayos de la aurora.

MANUEL ALTOLAGUIRRE

Mi Hermano Luis

Mi hermano Luis
me besaba dudando
en los andenes de las estaciones.
Me esperaba siempre
o me acompañaba para despedirme
y ahora,
cuando se me ha marchado no sé dónde,

Ultimate Death

I demand the ultimate death of this war
because I want to observe myself in the current
like some mauled and suffering body,
like a tree they strip of its fruits,
one whose branches they pull off
and make use of the wood from its trunk...

And if I'm not able to see myself,
if only roots are left of me,
if birds vainly search for
the site of their nests
in the sad absences of my limbs,
then, from the depths,
with the silence of a springtime,
insinuations of verdure and life
will sprout from the earth like weeping.
I'll be that multitude of adolescents,
that crown of laurel which encircles
the trunk brought down by the axe.
Multiplied life death brings.
Multiple are the rays of the dawn.

MANUEL ALTOLAGUIRRE

My Brother Luis

My brother Luis
would kiss me uncertainly
on the platforms of the stations.
He would always wait for me
or accompany me to bid farewell,
and now,
when he's left for I don't know where,

no llegué a tiempo,
no había nadie...
Ni siquiera el eco más remoto,
ni siquiera una sombra,
ni mi reflejo sobre las blancas nubes.
Este cielo es demasiado grande.
¿Dónde estarán los hijos de mi hermano?
¿Por qué no están aquí?
Yo iría con ellos
entre cosas reales.
Tal vez pudieran darme su retrato.
Yo no quiero que estén en una alcoba
con trajes negros.
Mejor será que corran por el río
que corran entre flores sin mirarlas,
como flores también,
como muchachos,
que no se paren nunca
como yo estoy parado
tan al borde del mar y de la muerte.

MANUEL ALTOLAGUIRRE

Elegía Española
1937

Dime, háblame
Tú, esencia misteriosa
De nuestra raza
Tras de tantos siglos,
Hálito creador
De los hombres hoy vivos,
A quienes veo labrados del odio
Hasta alzar con su esfuerzo
La muerte como paisaje de tu vida.

Cuando la antigua primavera
Vuelve a tejer su encanto

I didn't arrive in time,
there was no one there...
Not even the remotest echo,
not even a shadow,
nor my reflection upon the white clouds.
This sky is way too large.
Where could my brother's sons be?
Why aren't they here?
I would go with them
among real things.
Maybe they could give me his picture.
I don't want them to be in some bedroom
with black suits on.
It would be better if they ran along the river,
rather than run amid flowers without looking at them,
like flowers, also,
like young boys
who never stop
as I am stopped
so near the edge of the sea and death.

MANUEL ALTOLAGUIRRE

Spanish Elegy
1937

Tell me, speak to me,
You, mysterious essence
Of our race
After so many centuries,
Creative breath
Of men alive today,
Whom I see wrought by hate
Until hoisting death up by their spirited effort
Like a landscape of your life.

When the ancient springtime
Returns to weave its charm

Sobre tu cuerpo inmenso,
¿Cuál ave hallará nido
Y qué savia una rama
Donde brotar con verde impulso?
¿Qué rayo de la luz alegre,
Qué nube sobre el campo solitario,
Hallarán agua, cristal de viejo hogar en calma
Donde reflejen su irisado juego?

Háblame, madre;
Y al llamarte así, digo
Que ninguna mujer lo fué de nadie
Como tú lo eres mía.
Háblame, dime
Una sola palabra en estos lentos días,
En los días informes
Que frente a ti se esgrimen
Como amargo cuchillo
Entre las manos de tus propios hijos.

No te alejes así, ensimismada
Bajo los largos velos cenicientos
Que nos niegan tus anchos ojos bellos.
Esas flores caídas,
Pétalos rotos entre sangre y lodo,
En tus manos estaban luciendo eternamente
Desde siglos atrás, cuando mi vida
Era un sueño en la mente de los dioses.

Eres tú, son tus ojos lo que busca
Quien te llama luchando con la muerte,
A ti, remota y enigmática
Madre de tantas almas idas
Que te legaron, con un fulgor de clara piedra,
Su afán de eternidad cifrado en hermosura.

Pero no eres tan sólo
Dueña de afanes muertos;
Tierna, amorosa has sido con nuestro afán viviente,
Compasiva ante nuestra desdicha de efímeros.
¿Supiste acaso si de ti éramos dignos?

About your immense body,
Which bird will encounter a nest
And what sap a branch
On which to sprout with green impulse?
What ray of joyous light,
What cloud above the solitary field,
Will encounter water, glass of an old home at peace
Upon which to reflect their iridescent game?

Speak to me, mother,
And on calling you thus, I say
That no woman was so much a mother to anyone
As you are to me.
Speak to me, say
Just one word to me in these sluggish days,
In these shapeless days
That are fencing in front of you
Like a bitter knife
In the hands of your own children.

Do not draw away like that, lost in thought
Under those long ashen veils
That deny us your wide, lovely eyes.
Those fallen flowers,
Broken petals amid blood and mire,
Were eternally shining in your hands
Since centuries past, when my life
Was a dream in the mind of the gods.

It is you, your eyes he seeks,
He who calls out to you while battling with death,
To you, remote and enigmatic
Mother of so many departed souls
Who bequeathed you, with a brilliance of clear stone,
Their burning desire for eternity based upon beauty.

But you are not only
Mistress of dead desires;
Tender, loving you were with our living desire,
Compassionate before our misfortune of being ephemeral.
Did you learn, perhaps, whether we were worthy of you?

Contempla ahora a través de las lágrimas:
Mira cuántos traidores,
Mira cuántos cobardes
Lejos de ti en fuga vergonzosa,
Renegando tu nombre y tu regazo,
Cuando a tus pies, mientras la larga espera,
Si desde el suelo alzamos hacia ti la mirada
Tus hijos oscuramente sienten
La recompensa de estas horas fatídicas.

No sabe qué es la vida
Quien jamás alentó bajo la guerra.
Ella sobre nosotros sus densas alas cierne
Y oigo su silbo helado
Y veo los bruscos muertos
Caer sobre la hierba calcinada,
Mientras el cuerpo mío
Sufre y lucha con unos enfrente de esos otros.

No sé qué tiembla y muere en mí
Al verte así dolida y solitaria,
En ruinas los claros dones
De tus hijos a través de los siglos,
Porque mucho he amado tu pasado,
Resplandor victorioso entre sombra y olvido.

Tu pasado eres tú
Y al mismo tiempo eres
La aurora que aun no alumbra nuestros campos.
Tú sola sobrevives;
Aunque venga la muerte
Sólo en ti está la fuerza
De hacernos esperar a ciegas el futuro.

Que por encima de estos y esos muertos
Y encima de estos y esos vivos que combaten
Algo advirte que tú sufres con todos;
Y su odio, su crueldad, su lucha,
Ante ti vanos son como sus vidas,
Porque tú eres eterna
Y sólo los creaste
Para la paz y gloria de su estirpe.

Luis Cernuda

Now contemplate through your tears:
Observe how many traitors,
Observe how many cowards
Far from you in shameful flight,
Renouncing your name and your bosom,
While at your feet, during this long wait,
If we lift our eyes from the ground toward you,
Your children obscurely sense
The reward of these ominous hours.

He does not know what life is,
He who never drew breath in war.
Its dense wings hover over us,
And I hear its icy whistling
And I see these abrupt dead men
Falling upon the calcined grass
While this body of mine
Suffers and struggles with a few in front of those others.

I do not know what trembles and dies inside me
On seeing you pained and solitary like that,
The fair gifts of your children,
Throughout the centuries, in ruins,
Because I have greatly loved your past,
Victorious splendor amid shadow and oblivion.

You are your past
And at the same time you are
The dawn that does not as yet illuminate our fields.
You alone survive;
Although death may come,
Only within you is there the strength
To make us blindly await the future.

For despite these and those dead men,
And despite these and those of the living locked in combat,
Something is indicating that you suffer along with everyone;
And their hatred, their cruelty, their struggle,
Are vain in front of you, as are their lives,
Because you are eternal
And you created them only
For the peace and glory of their lineage.

LUIS CERNUDA

Elegía a la Luna de España

Vida tras vida fueron
Olvidando los hombres
Aquella diosa virgen
Que misteriosamente, desde el cielo,
Con amor apacible
Asiste a sus vigilias
En el dulce silencio de las noches.

Ella ha sido quien viera los abuelos
Remotos, cuando abordan
En sus pintados barcos,
Y ágiles y desnudos se apoderan
Con un trémulo imperio de esta tierra,
Así como el amante
Arrebata y penetra el cuerpo del amado.

Sus trabajos vió luego, sus cohabitaciones,
Y otros seres menudos,
Inhábiles, gritando entre los brazos
De los dominadores, y sus mujeres lánguidas
Sonreir débilmente a la raza naciente.

Miró sus largas guerras
Con pueblos enemigos
Y el azote sagrado
De luchas fratricidas;
Contempló esclavitudes y triunfos,
Prostituciones, crímenes,
Prosperidad, traiciones,
El sordo griterío,
Todo el horror humano que salva la hermosura,
Y con ella la calma,
La paz donde brota la historia.

También miró el arado
Con el siervo pasando
Sobre le antiguo campo de batalla,

Elegy to the Moon of Spain

Life after life men
Were forgetting
That virgin goddess
Who mysteriously, from the heavens,
With gentle love
Attends their vigils
In the sweet silence of the night.

She was the one to see those remote
Ancestors when they land
In their painted ships,
And agile and naked they take possession
Of this land with a tremulous arrogance,
In the same way a lover
Seizes and penetrates the body of his loved one.

Later she saw their works, their cohabitations,
And, also, other lesser beings,
Unfit ones, shouting in the arms
Of the dominators, and their languid women
Smile weakly upon this nascent race.

She observed their long wars
With enemy peoples
And the scourge
Of fratricidal struggles;
She contemplated slaveries and triumphs,
Prostitutions, crimes,
Prosperity, treacheries,
The deafening uproar,
All the human horror that is saved by beauty,
And with it, tranquillity,
That peace in which history blossoms.

She also observed the plow
Passing with the serf
Over the ancient battlefield,

Fertilizado por tanto cuerpo joven,
Y en ese mismo suelo ha visto cruzar luego
Al orgulloso dueño sobre recios caballos,
Mientras la hierba, ortiga y cardo
Brotaban por las vastas propiedades.

Cuánta sangre ha corrido
Ante el destino intacto de la diosa,
Cuánto semen viril
Vió surgir entre espasmos
De cuerpos hoy deshechos
En el polvo y el viento,
Cuyos eternos átomos con leves nubes grises
Velan al embeleso de vasta descendencia
Su tranquilo semblante compasivo.

Cuántas claras ruinas,
Con jaramago apenas adornadas,
Como fuertes castillos un día las ha visto;
Piedras más elocuentes que los siglos
Que hollara el paso leve
De esbeltas cazadoras, un neblí sobre el puño,
Oblicua la mirada soñolienta
Entre un aburrimiento y un amor clandestino.

Sombras, sombars efímeras,
En tanto ella, adolescente
Como en los prados de la edad de oro,
Vierte, azulada urna,
Su embeleso letal
Sobre nuevos cuerpos oscuros
Que la primavera enfebrece
Con agudos perfumes vegetales,

Allá, tras de las torres, un reflejo
Delata la presencia del mar,
Mientras los hombres solitarios duermen
Inermes en su lecho y confiados.
Los enemigos yacen confundidos;
Algo inmenso reposa, aunque la muerte aceche.
Y un mágico reflejo entre los árboles
Permite al soñador abandonarse al canto,
Al placer y al reposo,
Al lo que siendo efírmero se sueña como eterno.

Fertilized by so many young bodies,
And over this same ground she later saw
The proud master crossing on vigorous horses
While the grass, nettle and thistle
Grew throughout those vast estates.

How much blood has been shed
Before the unbroken destiny of the goddess,
How much virile semen
Did she see flowing amid the spasms
Of bodies today decomposed
In dust and the wind,
Whose eternal atoms with light, grey clouds
Veil, to the enchantment of a vast lineage,
Her tranquil and compassionate countenance.

How many clear ruins,
Barely adorned with mustard plants,
Did she see one day as strong castles,
Stones more eloquent than the centuries
That the light footstep of svelte huntresses
Was to tread upon, a falcon upon their fist,
Oblique their somnolent gaze,
Between boredom and clandestine love.

Shadows, ephemeral shadows,
Meanwhile, she, adolescent
As if in the meadows of the golden age,
Pours out, bluish urn,
Her lethal enchantment
Over new and obscure bodies
That the springtime enfevers
With pungent vegetal perfumes.

There, behind the towers, a reflection
Divulges the presence of the sea
While solitary men sleep
Unarmed in their beds and unsuspecting.
The enemies rest in disarray;
Something huge reposes, though death lies in ambush.
And a magical reflection amongst the trees
Allows the dreamer to abandon himself to song,
To pleasure and to repose,
To that though being ephemeral is dreamed of as eternal.

Murieron esperanzas y recuerdos,
La fe, porque los vivos ven morirse
La vida en ellos lentamente,
Arrastrándose lánguidos, tal un hermoso oro
Que antes para el mercado fuera útil,
Y una mano divina en el ocio lo adornara
Con fulgurantes piedras,
Vana y preciosa joya acompañando
El cuerpo hacia el olvido funerario
Como a la momia de jerarca poderoso.

Cuánta sombra ella ha visto surgir y ponerse,
Cuánto estío y otoño madurar y caer,
Cuántas aguas pasar de las nubes
A la tierra, de los ríos al mar,
Cuántos hombres ha visto desear y morir
Y renacer su eterno anhelo
En otros y otros y otros labios.

Mas una noche, al contemplar la antigua
Morada de los hombres, sólo ha de ver allá
El reflejo de su dulce fulgor,
Mudo y vacío entonces,
Estéril tal su hermosura virginal;
Sin que ningunos ojos humanos
Hasta ella se alcen a través de las lágrimas,
Definitivamente frente a frente
El silencio de un mundo que ha sido
Y la pura belleza tranquila de la nada.

LUIS CERNUDA

Despedida de un Año
(1936)

Dentro de breves horas
habrás partido para siempre,
como un barco fantasma que se aleja

Hopes and memories died,
And faith, because the living see life
Dying slowly within themselves,
Crawling languidly along, like a beautiful gold piece
That before was of use in the marketplace,
And a hand, divine in its pleasure, adorned it
With sparkling stones,
A vain and precious jewel accompanying
The corpse toward that funeral oblivion
Like the mummy of a powerful hierarch.

How much shadow has she seen arise and vanish,
How much summer and autumn ripen and fall,
How many waters pass from the clouds
To the earth, from the rivers to the sea,
In how many men has she seen her eternal yearning
Desired and die and be reborn
Upon the lips of others and others and others.

But one night, on contemplating the ancient
Dwelling place of men, only the reflection
Of her sweet brilliance, mute and empty then,
Is to be seen there,
Sterile like her virginal beauty;
Without any human eyes
Raised toward her through the tears,
The silence of a world that has been
And the pure, tranquil beauty of nothingness
Are once and for all face to face.

LUIS CERNUDA

Farewell to a Year
(1936)

Within a few hours
you will have departed forever,
like some ghost ship receding

hacia el confín sin árboles
donde la tierra pierde sus dominios.
Soltarás las amarras
sacudido por una tempestad imprevista,
y lanzando un silencio ensordecedor
irás a buscar esa teoría del tiempo
que aclamará tu llegada inmortal,
con los ojos impávidos
por el horror de tu vida reciente.
Eres aún el halo que se escapa de nuestras bocas,
el impalpable curador de las heridas.
Unas horas tan sólo y no serás
este delgado aire que evaporan los ríos,
el día venidero que asiste a las penosas realidades
tendido en muelles huertos,
ni tu nombre designará
a la inmensa muchedumbre que se agita
por un suelo encrespado.
¡Oh tiempo, pronto a despeñarse sobre el abismo!
Tus colmadas bodegas de sangre,
las víctimas inmoladas en tu seno,
las hecatombes que ahogan tu garganta
con un crudo espesor de humo negro,
dejan de ser la vida encarnizada,
pasan a ser los hechos,
y un sutil resplandor los alumbra
cuando tus pies ligeros
dan el postrero paso decisivo
al final de los montes.
Loor a ti, demoledor insensible,
por cuyas jornadas turbulentas
la intensa melancolía coronada de adormideras
huye gimiendo al son de las ruinas.
Loor a ti, que has sabido dejar como libre
el parado corazón de los hombres.
Tu definitiva noche se cierne sobre la tierra,
y los luchadores en las frías avanzadas
por segunda vez te piensan
como un ser mágico que ahora se desvanece
arrancando de la realidad
una última vagoneta de cadáveres.
Loor a ti, sin embargo,
que, con espada de fuego y pecho de piedra,

towards that treeless boundary
where the earth loses its dominion.
Jolted about by some unexpected tempest,
you will throw off the mooring lines,
and letting loose with a deafening silence,
you will go off in search of that theory of time
which will acclaim your immortal arrival,
your eyes undaunted
by the horror of your recent past.
You are still that halo escaping from our mouths,
that impalpable healer of wounds.
Just a few more hours and you will not be
this thin air that evaporated rivers,
or that coming day which attends the painful realities
hanging in luxurious gardens,
nor will your name serve as one
for that immense multitude who agitate
upon an enraged soil.
Oh, time, soon to hurl yourself over the abyss!
Your overflowing wine cellars of blood,
the victims immolated in your breast,
the hecatombs that suffocate your throat
with a crude density of black smoke,
are ceasing to be life incarnate
and are passing on to become deeds,
and a subtle radiance illuminates them
when your light feet
take that final, decisive step
at the end of the mountains.
Praise to you, insensitive wrecker,
through whose turbulent days
this intense melancholy crowned with opium poppies
flees, wailing to the sound of the ruins.
Praise to you who knew how to set free
this stopped heart of men.
Your ultimate night hovers over the earth,
and for a second time
the combatants in their cold outposts think of you
as some magic being who now vanishes,
wrenching from reality
one last flatcar of cadavers.
Praise to you, nevertheless,
for, with fiery sword and chest of stone,

asistirás en el umbral
a esta era en que mi país
inicia su esperanza de continuidad
sobre sus campos abandonados,
sobre sus ciudades deshechas.

Noche, diciembre, 1936.

JUAN GIL-ALBERT

Recoged Esta Voz

I

Naciones de la tierra, patrias del mar, hermanos
del mundo y de la nada:
habitantes perdidos y lejanos,
más que del corazón, de la mirada.

Aquí tengo una voz enardecida,
aquí tengo una vida combatida y airada,
aquí tengo un rumor, aquí tengo una vida.

Abierto estoy, mirad, como una herida.
Hundido estoy, mirad, estoy hundido
en medio de mi pueblo y de sus males.
Herido voy, herido y malherido,
sangrando por trincheras y hospitales.

Hombres, mundos, naciones,
atended, escuchad mi sangrante sonido,
recoged mis latidos de quebranto
en vuestros espaciosos corazones,
porque yo empuño el alma cuando canto.

Cantando me defiendo
y defiendo mi pueblo cuando en mi pueblo imprimen
su herradura de pólvora y estruendo
los bárbaros del crimen.

you will be present in the threshold
of this era in which my country
initiates its expectation of continuity
over its abandoned fields,
over its destroyed cities.

Night, December 1936.

JUAN GIL-ALBERT

Gather This Voice

I

Nations of the earth, homelands of the sea, brothers
of the world and nothingness:
inhabitants, lost and far
from our view, more than from our hearts.

Here I have an inflamed voice,
here I have an embattled and angered life,
here I have a murmur, here I have a life.

Open I am, look, like a wound.
Submerged I am, look, I'm submerged
in the midst of my people and their ills.
Wounded I go, wounded and badly wounded,
bleeding through trenches and hospitals.

Men, worlds, nations,
pay heed, listen to my bloodied sound,
gather my grieving heartbeats together
in your spacious hearts,
for I grasp my soul when I sing.

Singing I defend myself
and I defend my people when the barbarians
of this crime imprint their horseshoe
of thunder and gunpowder upon my people.

Esta es su obra, esta:
pasan, arrasan como torbellinos,
y son ante su cólera funesta
armas los horizontes y muerte los caminos.

El llanto que por valles y balcones se vierte,
en las piedras diluvia y en las piedras trabaja,
y no hay espacio para tanta muerte,
y no hay madera para tanta caja.

Caravanas de cuerpos abatidos.
Todo vendajes, penas y pañuelos:
todo camillas donde a los heridos
se les quiebran las fuerzas y los vuelos.

Sangre, sangre por árboles y suelos,
sangre por aguas, sangre por paredes,
y un temor de que España se desplome
del peso de la sangre que moja entre sus redes
hasta el pan que se come.

Recoged este viento,
naciones, hombres, mundos,
que parte de las bocas de conmovido aliento
y de los hospitales moribundos.

Aplicad las orejas
a mi clamor de pueblo atropellado,
al ¡ay! de tantas madres, a las quejas
de tanto ser luciente que el luto ha devorado.

Los pechos que empujaban y herían las montañas,
vedlos desfallecidos sin leche ni hermosura,
y ved las blancas novias y las negras pestañas
caídas y sumidas en uns siesta obscura.

Aplicad la pasion de las entrañas
a este pueblo que muere con un gesto invencible
sembrado por los labios y la frente,
bajo los implacables aeroplanos
que arrebatan terrible,
terrible, ignominiosa, diariamente,
a las madres los hijos de las manos.

This is their work, this:
they pass by, razing like whirlwinds,
and, in front of their fatal wrath,
the horizons are weapons and the roads, death.

The weeping that pours through valleys and balconies
deluges the stones and upon the stones it works,
and there isn't space for so much death
and there isn't wood for so many boxes.

Caravans of dejected bodies.
Everything bandages, suffering and handkerchiefs:
everything stretchers where the strength
and flights of the wounded are broken.

Blood, blood on trees and ground,
blood upon the waters, blood on the walls,
and a dread that Spain will topple over
from the weight of the blood that soaks through its nets
right down to the bread that is eaten.

Nations, men, worlds,
gather together this wind
that departs these mouths of heartfelt breath
and these moribund hospitals.

Apply your ears
to my clamor of a trampled people,
to the "oh!" of so many mothers, to the outcries
of so many bright beings mourning has devoured.

Breasts that would push and wound the mountains,
look at them now without milk or beauty,
and view the white brides and their black eyelashes,
fallen and submerged in an obscure nap.

Apply the passion of your entrails
to this people that dies with an invincible gesture
sown by lips and brow,
beneath those implacable aeroplanes
that seize terribly,
terribly, ignominiously, daily,
children from the hands of their mothers.

Ciudades de trabajo y de inocencia,
juventudes que brotan de la encina,
troncos de bronce, cuerpos de potencia
yacen precipitados en la ruina.

Un porvenir de polvo se avecina,
se avecina un suceso
en que no quedará ninguna cosa:
ni piedra sobre piedra ni hueso sobre hueso.

España no es España, que es una inmensa fosa,
que es un gran cementerio rojo y bombardeado:
los bárbaros la quieren de este modo.

Será la tierra un denso corazón desolado,
si vosotros, naciones, hombres, mundos,
con mi pueblo del todo
y vuestro pueblo encima del costado,
no quebráis los colmillos iracundos.

II

Pero no lo será: que un mar piafante,
triunfante siempre, siempre decidido,
hecho para la luz, para la hazaña,
agita su cabeza de rebelde diamante,
bate su pie calzado en el sonido
por todos los cadáveres de España.

Es una juventud: recoged este viento.
Su sangre es el cristal que no se empaña,
su sombrero el laurel y el pedernal su aliento.

Donde clava la fuerza de sus dientes
brota un volcán de diáfanas espadas,
y sus hombros batientes,
y sus talones guían llamaradas.

Está compuesta de hombres de trabajo:
de herreros rojos, de albos albañiles,
de yunteros con rostro de cosechas.

Cities of work and innocence,
generations of youth sprouting from the oaks,
trunks of bronze, bodies of power
rest there rushed into ruin.

An expectation of gunpowder approaches,
some incident is approaching
in which nothing will be left:
not stone upon stone nor bone upon bone.

Spain is not Spain, it's an immense grave,
it's a large red and bombarded cemetery:
the barbarians want it that way.

The earth will become a dense and desolate heart,
if you, nations, men, worlds,
with the whole of my people
and with your people on our flanks,
don't break their wrathful fangs.

II

But that won't be: for a stomping sea,
triumphant always, always resolute,
made for the light, for heroic exploit,
shakes its head of rebellious diamond,
pounds its shod foot on the sound
for all the cadavers of Spain.

It's a generation of youth: gather this wind.
Their blood is the glass that never fogs;
their hat, the laurel; and flint, their life's breath.

Wherever they afix the force of their teeth,
a volcano of transparent swords erupts,
their shoulders swinging,
their heels shooting flames.

It's composed of men who work:
of red blacksmiths, albescent masons,
plowmen with harvest faces.

Oceánicamente transcurren por debajo
de un fragor de sirenas y herramientas fabriles
y de gigantes arcos alumbrados con flechas.

A pesar de la muerte, estos varones
con metal y relámpagos igual que los escudos,
hacen retroceder a los cañones
acobardados, temblorosos, mudos.

El polvo no los puede y hacen del polvo fuego,
savia, explosión, verdura repentina:
con su poder de abril apasionado
precipitan el alma del espliego,
el parto de la mina,
el fértil movimiento del arado.

Ellos harán de cada ruina un prado,
de cada pena un fruto de alegría,
de España un firmamento de hermosura.
Vedlos agigantar el mediodía
y hermosearlo todo con su joven bravura.

Se merecen la espuma de los truenos,
se merecen la vida y el olor del olivo,
los españoles amplios y serenos
que mueven la mirada como un pájaro altivo.

Naciones, hombres, mundos, esto escribo:
la juventud de España saldrá de las trincheras
de pie, invencible como la semilla,
pues tiene un alma llena de banderas
que jamás se somete ni arrodilla.

Allá van por los yermos de Castilla
los cuerpos que parecen potros batalladores,
toros de victorioso desenlace,
diciéndose en us sangre de generosas flores
que morir es la cosa más grande que se hace.

Quedarán en el tiempo vencedores,
siempre de sol y majestad cubiertos,
los guerreros de huesos tan gallardos

Oceanically they pass time beneath
a din of sirens and manufacturing tools
and gigantic arcs illuminated with arrows.

Despite death, these males,
with metal and lightning just like shields,
make the cannons draw back
intimidated, trembling, silenced.

Powder was no match for them and out of it they make fire,
sap, explosion, sudden greenness:
with the power of their impassioned flower of youth
they precipitate the soul of the lavender,
the product of the mine,
the fertile movement of the plow.

They will make a meadow out of each ruin;
out of each sorrow, a fruit of happiness;
out of Spain, a firmament of beauty.
Look at them making the midday gigantic
and beautifying it with their youthful bravery.

They deserve the foam of thunderclaps,
they deserve life and the scent of the olive tree,
these ample and serene Spaniards
who glance about like a proud bird.

Nations, men, worlds, this I write:
the youth of Spain will leave the trenches
on foot, invincible like the seed,
for they have a soul filled with banners
that never submits nor falls to its knees.

There over the barren plains of Castile travel
these bodies that seem to be battling colts,
bulls of victorious outcome,
expressing with their blood of generous flowers
that dying is the greatest thing one can do.

In time they will be left the victors,
forever covered in sun and majesty,
these warriors of such gallant bones,

que si son muertos son gallardos muertos:
la juventud que a España salvará, aunque tuviera
que combatir con un fusil de nardos
y una escopeta de cera.

(Madrid, 15 de enero de 1937).

MIGUEL HERNANDEZ

El Niño Yuntero

Carne de yugo, ha nacido
más humillado que bello,
con el cuello perseguido
por el yugo para el cuello.

Nace como la herramienta
a los golpes destinado
de una tierra descontenta
y un insatisfecho arado.

Entre estiércol puro y vivo
de vacas, trae a la vida
un alma color de olivo
vieja ya y encallecida.

Empieza a vivir y empieza
a morir de punta a punta
levantando la corteza
de su madre con la yunta.

Empieza a sentir y siente
la vida como una guerra
y a dar fatigosamente
en los huesos de la tierra.

Contar sus años no sabe
y ya sabe que el sudor

for if they're dead men, they're gallant dead men:
these youths will save Spain, even if they have
to fight with a rifle of nards
and a shotgun of wax.

Madrid, January 15, 1937.

MIGUEL HERNANDEZ

The Plowboy

Flesh for the yoke, born
more humiliated than handsome,
with his neck pursued
by the yoke for his neck.

Born like the tool,
destined for the blows
of a discontented land
and an unsatisfied plow.

Amid the pure and strong cow
dung, he brings to the life
an olive-colored soul,
old already and calloused.

He begins to live and begins
to die, from top to bottom,
lifting that crust
of his mother with the team.

He begins to feel and feels
this life as if it were a war
and he strikes wearily upon
the bones of the earth.

Count his years he knows not
and yet he knows that sweat

es una corona grave
de sal para el labrador.

A fuerza de golpes fuertes
y a fuerza de sol bruñido
con una ambición de muerte
despedaza un pan reñido.

Trabaja y mientras trabaja
masculinamente serio
se unge de lluvia y se alhaja
de carne de cementerio.

Cada nuevo día es
más raíz, menos criatura,
que escucha bajo sus pies
la voz de la sepultura.

Y como raíz se hunde
en la tierra lentamente
para que la tierra inunde
de paz y panes su frente.

Me duele este niño hambriento
como una grandiosa espina,
y su vivir ceniciento
revuelve mi alma de encina.

Le veo arar los rastrojos,
y devorar un mendrugo,
y declarar con los ojos
que por qué es carne de yugo.

Me da su arado en el pecho
y su vida en la garganta,
y sufro viendo el barbecho
tan grande bajo su planta.

¿Quién salvará este chiquillo
menor que un grano de avena?
¿De dónde saldrá el martillo
verdugo de esta cadena?

is a grave crown of salt
for the farm laborer.

By dint of his strong blows
and because of the polished sun,
he rips apart with deathly ambition
a hard-fought-for loaf of bread.

He works and while he works,
masculinely serious,
he is anointed with rain
and adorned with cemetery flesh.

Each new day he becomes
more root, less infant,
for he hears that call
of the grave under his feet.

And like the root he sinks
slowly down into the ground,
so that the earth is flooded
in peace and his brow with bread.

This hungry child pains me
just like an enormous thorn
and his ashen-colored life
disturbs my soul of oak.

I see him plow the stubble
and devour a scrap of bread
and declare with his eyes,
why is he flesh for the yoke?

His plow strikes me in the heart
and his life in my throat,
and I suffer seeing the fallow
so large beneath his sole.

Who will save this little boy,
smaller than a grain of oats?
From where will the hammer come,
that executioner of this chain?

Que salga del corazón
de los hombres jornaleros,
que antes de ser hombres son
y han sido niños yunteros.

La Insignia

Aquí,
por primera vez,
por una vez siquiera,
aquí, en la gran mesa de los grandes negocios del
    mundo,
aquí, en la gran mesa de los grandes negocios del
    hombre,
aquí, en estas alturas solitarias,
aquí, donde se oye sin descanso la voz milenaria
de los vientos,
de la arcilla,
y del agua
que nos ha ido formando a todos los hombres;
aquí, donde no llega el desgañitado vocerío de la
    propaganda mercenaria;
aquí, donde no tiene resuello ni vida el asma de los
    diplomáticos;
aquí, donde los comediantes de la Sociedad de
    Naciones no tienen papel;
aquí, bajo las estrellas,
alumbrados por las estrellas
y ante la Historia,
aquí, aquí,
colocad aquí
el gran problema del NEGOCIO ESPAÑOL.
Aquí, ante la Historia grande,
ante la Epica,
la otra, la otra historia,
la historia doméstica,
la historia nacional,

Let it come from the hearts
of these day-laboring men,
who before becoming men
are and have been plowboys.

MIGUEL HERNANDEZ

The Insignia

Here,
for the first time,
for even one time,
here, at the great table of these great business transactions
   of the world,
here, at the great table of these great business transactions
   of man,
here, in these solitary heights,
here, where one hears without stop the millenary voice
of the winds,
of the clay,
and of the water
that went about forming all men;
here, where that shrieked-out clamor of mercenary propaganda
   doesn't reach;
here, where the asthma of diplomats doesn't have
   breath or life;
here, where the comedians from the League of Nations
   don't have any part;
here, beneath the stars,
illuminated by the stars
and in front of History,
here, here,
place here
the big problem of SPANISH BUSINESS TRANSACTIONS.
Here, before great History,
before Epic Poetry,
is the other one, the other history,
the domestic history,
the national history,

97

la que nuestro orgullo de gusanos enseña a los niños
   de las escuelas,
no es más que un registro de mentiras
y un índice de crímines y de vanidades.
Aquí, aquí,
frente a la Epica,
frente a la Historia verdadera,
colocad aquí
EL NEGOCIO ESPAÑOL.
Y venid los poetas del mundo,
todos los poetas del mundo,
todos los poetas verdaderos del mundo.
(Poetas con el signo épico y activo
que aquí hemos dado a la palabra y al oficio),
los poetas de todas las naciones,
los poetas de todos los pueblos.
De los pueblos grandes
y de los pueblos pequeños;
de los pueblos blancos,
de los pueblos negros
y de los pueblos amarillos;
de los que comen con manteca
y de los que comen con aceite;
de los que beben vino,
de los que beben té,
de los que beben cerveza,
de los que beben en todas las fuentes
y comen en todas las mesas
pero que aún tienen hambre y sed de justicia...
Poetas de todas las latitudes:
venid aquí,
subid aquí,
aquí, aquí, aquí,
donde no pueden llegar los políticos,
ni el burgués,
ni el banquero,
ni el arzobispo,
ni el comerciante,
ni el aristócrata degenerado,
ni el bufón,
ni el mendigo,
ni el cobarde.
Aquí, aquí,

the one our worm-like pride teaches the children
    in the schools,
it's nothing more than a register of lies
and an index of crimes and vanities.
Here, here,
facing Epic Poetry,
facing the real History,
place here
SPANISH BUSINESS TRANSACTIONS.
And come, poets of the world,
all the poets of the world,
all the true poets of the world.
(Poets with an epic and active sign
that here we've given to the word and the craft),
poets of all nations,
poets of all peoples.
From large lands
and from small lands;
from the white peoples,
from the black peoples
and from the yellow peoples;
from the lands that eat with butter
and from those that eat with oil;
from those that drink wine,
from those that drink tea,
from those that drink beer,
from those that drink from all the fountains
and eat at all the tables
but still have a hunger and thirst for justice...
Poets from all the latitudes:
come here,
climb up here,
here, here, here,
where the politicians can't reach,
or the bourgeois,
or the banker,
or the archbishop,
or the merchant,
or the degenerate aristocrat,
or the buffoon,
or the beggar,
or the coward.
Here, here,

frente a la Historia,
frente a la Historia grande,
bajo la luz de las estrellas,
sobre la tierra prístina y eterna del mundo
y en la presencia misma de Dios,
aquí,
vamos a hablar aquí
del NEGOCIO ESPAÑOL REVOLUCIONARIO.
Hay dos Españas:
la de formas
y la de esencias.
La de las formas que se desgastan
y la de las esencias eternas.
La de las formas que mueren
y la de las esencias que comienzan a organizarse de
    nuevo.
En la España de las formas desgastadas
están los símbolos obliterados,
los ritos sin sentido,
los uniformes inflados,
las medallas sin leyenda,
los hombres huecos,
los cuerpos de serrín,
el ritmo doméstico y sonámbulo,
las exégesis farisaicas,
el verso vano
y la oración muerta que van contando las avellanas
    horadadas de los rosarios.
Dios, la fuerza creadora del mundo,
se ha ido de esa España
y todo se ha quedado sin sustancia.
Nuestra morada nacional entonces
es una cueva donde ordena la avaricia,
y los privilegios de la avaricia.
Es la época de los raposos.
Y los pueblos de Historia tan pura como el nuestro
no son ya más que madrigueras
donde los raposos amontonan su rapiña.
En la España de las esencias que quieren organizarse
    de nuevo,
están las ráfagas primeras que mueven las entrañas
    nacionales,

facing History,
facing great History,
beneath the light from the stars,
over the pristine and eternal soil of the world
and in the very presence of God,
here,
let's speak here
about these REVOLUTIONARY TRANSACTIONS OF SPAIN.
There are two Spains:
one of forms
and one of essences.
One of forms that wear out
and one of eternal essences.
One of forms that die
and one of essences that are beginning to organize
    themselves anew.
In the Spain of the worn-out forms
there are obliterated symbols,
senseless rites,
inflated uniforms,
legendless medals,
hollow men,
sawdust bodies,
that domestic and somnambulistic rhythm,
pharisaical exegesis,
vain verse
and the dead prayer with which they count the bored-out
    hazel nuts of the rosaries.
God, the creative force of the world,
has departed that Spain
and everything was left without substance.
Our national abode, therefore,
is a cave where greed is ordained,
and the privileges of that greed.
It's the epoch of foxes.
And those lands with a History as pure as ours
now are nothing more than hideouts
where the foxes pile up their pillage.
In Spain of the essences that want to organize
    themselves anew,
are the first gusts of wind that move our national
    entrails,

los huracanes incontrolables que sacuden la substancia
    dormida,
la substancia prístina de que está hecho el árbol, y
    el cuerpo del hombre.
Y están también los terremotos que rompen la tierra,
desgarran la carne,
desbordan los ríos
y las arterias de nuestro anatomía
para dar salida al espíritu encadenado
y mostrarle su camino hacia la renovación y hacia
    la luz.

Es la época de los héroes.
De los héroes contra los raposos.
Es la época en que todo se deforma y se revuelve;
las exégesis se cambian del revés,
los presagios de los grandes poetas se hacen
    realidad,
aparecen nuevos Cristos.
Y las viejas parábolas evangélicas se escapan de la
    ingenua retórica de los versículos, para venirse a
    mover y a organizar nuestra vida.

Ahí están, ¡Miradlas!
Ahí están en el aire todavía,
temblando de emoción,
cruzando los cielos desde hace veinte siglos,
en la curva evangélica de una parábola poética,
estas palabras revolucionarias,
estas palabras comunistas,
estas palabras anarquistas:
"Es más fácil que pase un camello por el ojo de
    una aguja, que entre un rico en el reino de los
    cielos."
Los curas las han estado
escupiendo,
vomitando desde los púlpitos,
centuria tras centuria,
año tras año,
domingo tras domingo.
Los prelados y los obispos las han llevado
de catedral en catedral,
de iglesia en iglesia,

the uncontrollable hurricanes which shake that sleeping
    substance,
that pristine substance from which the tree is made,
    and the body of man.
And also the earthquakes that break the ground up,
rip the flesh apart,
make the rivers
and the arteries of our national anatomy overflow
in order to provide an exit for our enchained spirit
and show it the way towards renovation and towards
    the light.

It's the epoch of heroes.
Of heroes against the foxes.
It's the epoch in which everything is deformed and stirred up;
the exegeses are turned inside out,
the omens of the great poets become
    reality,
new Christs appear.
And the old evangelical parables escape the
    naive rhetoric of the versicles, in order to
    come here to move and to organize our life.

There they are. Look at them!
There they are still in the air,
trembling with emotion,
crossing the heavens for more than twenty centuries,
along the evangelic curve of a poetic parable,
these revolutionary words,
these communist words,
these anarchist words:
"It is easier for a camel to go through the eye of a
    needle, than for a rich man to enter into the kingdom
    of God."
The priests have been
spitting them out,
vomiting them from their pulpits,
century after century,
year after year,
Sunday after Sunday.
The prelates and bishops have taken them
from cathedral to cathedral,
from church to church,

de plática en plática,
y han acabado siempre por sentarse, despúes de los
	sermones, a la mesa de este rico de tan dudosa
	salvación, para decirle así, de una manera
	abierta y paladina:
El Evangelio no es más que una manera lírica de
	hablar.
Metáforas,
metáforas retóricas.
Retórica todo.
Metáforas hechas sólo para adornar el sermón
	melífluo y dominical de los predicadores
	elegantes.
¿Qué otra cosa podría ser?—dice el raposo.
¿Qué otra cosa podría ser?—dice el hombre
	doméstico.
Pero he aquí que llegan ahora unos hombres
	extraños,
los revolucionarios españoles,
los anarquistas ibéricos,
el Hombre heroico que dice: No hay retóricas;
el Hombre heroico que dice:
el verbo lírico de Cristo y de todos los poetas no es
	una quimera,
es un índice luminoso que nos invita a la acción y
	al heroísmo,
y esta metáfora del camello y de la aguja,
del pobre y del rico,
tiene un sentido que, desentrañado y realizado, puede
	llenar, si no de alegría, de dignidad la vida del
	hombre.
Esta es la exégesis heroica,
la exégesis anarquista,
la exégesis comunista,
la exégesis revolucionaria.
Escuchad:
Hay que salvar al rico.
Hay que salvarle de la dictadura de su riqueza,
porque debajo de sus riquezas
hay un hombre que tiene que entrar en el reino de
	los cielos,
en el reino de los héroes.

from sermon to sermon,
and they've always wound up sitting down, after
    their sermons, at the table of some rich man of such doubtful
    salvation, and say to him like this, in an open and
    manifest way:
The Gospel is nothing more than a *lyric* manner of
    speaking.
Metaphors,
rhetorical metaphors.
All of it rhetoric.
Metaphors made only to adorn the mellifluous
    and dominical sermon of these elegant
    preachers.
What else could it be? says the fox.
What else could it be? says the domestic
    man.
But here we have some strange men now
    arriving,
Spanish revolutionaries,
Iberian anarchists,
the heroic Man who says: There aren't any rhetorics;
the heroic Man who says:
the lyric word of Christ, and of all poets, isn't
    a chimera,
it's a luminous index that invites us to action and
    to heroism,
and that metaphor of the camel and the needle,
of the rich man and the poor man,
has a meaning, once deciphered and fulfilled, that can
    fill the life of man, if not with joy, then with
    dignity.
This is the heroic exegesis,
the anarchist exegesis,
the communist exegesis,
the revolutionary exegesis.
Listen:
The rich man has to be saved.
He has to be saved from the dictatorship of his riches,
because beneath his riches
there is a man who must enter the realm of
    the heavens,
the realm of heroes.

Pero también hay que salvar al pobre.
Porque debajo de la tiranía de su pobreza
hay otro hombre que ha nacido para héroe también.
Hay que salvar al rico y al pobre.
Hay que matar al rico y al pobre para que nazca el
    HOMBRE,
el hombre heroico.
El hombre, el hombre heroico es lo que importa.
Ni el rico,
ni el pobre,
ni el proletario,
ni el diplomático,
ni el industrial,
ni el comerciante,
ni el soldado,
ni el artista,
ni el poeta siquiera, en su sentido ordinario importan
    nada.
Nuestro oficio no es nuestro destino.
Nuestra profesión no es lo substantivo.
No hay otro oficio ni empleo que aquel que enseña
al mozo a ser un héroe.
El hombre heroico es lo que cuenta.
El hombre ahí,
desnudo,
bajo la noche,
y frente al misterio;
con su tragedia a cuestas,
con su verdadera tragedia,
con su única tragedia.
La que surge
cuando preguntamos,
cuando gritamos en al viento:
¿Quién soy yo?
Y el viento no responde
y no responde nadie.
¿Quién soy yo?... Silencio... Silencio...
Ni un eco... ni un signo...
Silencio.
Para que grite conmigo, busco yo al rico y le digo:
deja tus riquezas y ven aquí a gritar.
Para que grite conmigo, busco yo al pobre y le digo:
salva tu pobreza y ven aquí a gritar.

But the poor man also has to be saved.
Because beneath the tyranny of his poverty
there is another man who was also born to be a hero.
The rich man and the poor man have to be saved.
The rich man and the poor man must be killed so that
   MAN can be born,
the heroic man.
Man, heroic man is what's important.
Not the rich man,
not the poor man,
not the proletarian,
not the diplomant,
not the industrialist,
not the merchant,
not the soldier,
not the artist,
not even the poet, for in their ordinary sense they
   don't matter at all.
Our craft is not our destiny.
Our profession isn't the substinant thing.
There isn't another craft or job other than teaching
a lad to be a hero.
Heroic man is what counts.
That man there,
naked,
beneath the night
and facing the mystery;
with his tragedy upon his back,
with his true tragedy,
with his only tragedy.
The one that arises
when we ask,
when we shout into the wind:
Who am I?
And the wind doesn't respond,
and nobody responds.
Who am I?....Silence...Silence...
Not an echo...not a sign...
Silence.
So he'll shout with me, I search for the rich man and tell him:
leave your riches and come hear and shout.
So he'll shout with me, I search for the poor man and tell him:
overcome your poverty and come here and shout.

Todas las lenguas en un grito único
y todas las manos en un ariete solo,
para derribar la noche
y echar de nosotros la sombra.
No hay dictaduras humanas.
Estrella,
sólo estrellas,
estrellas dictadoras nos gobiernan.
Pero contra la dictadura de las estrellas,
la dictadura del heroísmo.
Y si la estrellas dicen:
siempre habrá pobres y ricos,
y el pez grande se come al chico;
contra la palabra de las estrellas,
el esfuerzo del heroísmo colectivo.
Para que grite conmigo contra los designios estelares
    busco yo al hombre,
para que junte conmigo su angustia y la funda con
    la mía en una sola voz, busco yo al hombre.
Esta es la exégesis heroica,
esta es la exégesis heroica, que tan bien le va al
    español,
al español revolucionario,
al comunista español,
al anarquista ibérico,
al anarquista angélico y adámico,
para quien la vida no es ni ha sido nunca
una cuestión de felicidad,
sino una cuestión de heroísmo.
Y su sangre,
esa sangre que está vertiendo ahora,
y la que ha vertido al través de la Historia,
no se pude medir con un criterio pragmático.

Esta es la exégesis heroica.
En cuanto se ha definido como doctrina
y ha adquirido posibilidades de realidad,
el mundo doméstico de los fariseos,
y la avaricia de los raposos
se han vuelto furiosos contra ella.
Y ahora,
ahora no hay más que una lucha enconada entre dos
    clases de hombres:

Every language in one single shout
and every hand upon one lone battering ram,
to demolish the night
and cast this shadow from us.
There aren't any humane dictatorships.
Star,
only stars,
dictator stars govern us.
But against the dictatorship of the stars,
the dictatorship of heroism.
And if the stars say:
there will always be rich and poor,
and the big fish eats the small one;
against the word of the stars,
the force of collective heroism.
So he'll shout along with me against these stellar designs,
    I search for man,
so he'll join his anguish to me and fuse it with
    mine in one single voice, I search for man.
This is the heroic exegesis,
this is the heroic exegesis that suits the Spaniard
    so well,
the revolutionary Spaniard,
the Spanish communist,
the Iberian anarchist,
the angelic and adamic anarchist,
for whom life is not nor ever has been
a question of happiness,
but rather one of heroism.
And his blood,
that blood he's now shedding,
and the one he's shed throughout history,
can't be measured by pragmatic criteria.

This is the heroic exegesis.
No sooner has it been defined as doctrine
and has acquired the possibility of becoming reality,
then the domestic world of the pharisees
and the greed of the foxes
turned furiously against it.
And now,
now there's nothing more than this embittering struggle
    between two classes of men:

la de los que quieren seguir la curva lírica de esta
    parábola en el cielo,
hasta sus últimas posibles realidades,
hasta verla caer en la tierra y moverse aún, abriéndole
    caminos nuevos al hombre por la Historia...
y la de los que aseguran que interpretar así la
    parábola es una blasfemia y una herejía.
Somos los viejos herejes del mundo,
contra los eternos fariseos,
contra los raposos que amontonan la rapiña detrás
    de las puertas.
Y no buscamos la felicidad.
Camaradas,
españoles revolucionarios,
comunistas ibéricos,
anarquistas adámicos y angélicos,
un día
tendremos ya pan y ocio,
y ya no habrá hambre ni prisas en el mundo.
Pero no seremos felices tampoco.
No hay posadas de felicidad
ni de descanso.
Se va siempre por un camino heroico hacia la
    dignidad y la superación de la vida.
Se cambiarán de sitio nuestras llagas,
nos dolerá otra carne,
y de sierras más frías bajará nuestro llanto.
Un día,
aquel mendigo chino
ya no estará a la puerta del hotel
golpeando allí por una rebanada de pan,
estará en al pirámide,
en la giba más alta de la Sierra Madre,
golpeando en el cielo,
en la puerta del cielo,
en el pecho de Dios,
por una rebanada de luz.

        .   .   .

Esta es mi palabra.
Y la tuya también.
La vieja palabra de todos los poetas del mundo,
de todos los poetas del mundo,

those who want to follow the lyric curve of this
    parable in the heavens
to its ultimate possible realities,
until seeing it fall to earth and, still moving, open up
    new paths through History to man...
and those who assure us that interpreting the parable
    in such a way is blasphemy and heresy.
We're the old heretics of the world,
against the eternal pharisees,
against the foxes that pile the plunder up behind
    their doors.
And we aren't looking for happiness.
Comrades,
revolutionary Spaniards,
Iberian communists,
adamic and angelic anarchists,
one day
we'll have bread and leisure,
and then there won't be any hunger or urgencies in the world.
But we won't be happy either.
There aren't any inns of happiness
or for rest.
Everything travels along a heroic route towards
    dignity and the surmounting of life.
Our open wounds will change places,
another flesh will pain us,
and our weeping will descend from the coldest sierras.
One day
that Chinese beggar
will no longer be there at the door of the hotel
knocking for a slice of bread,
he'll be on the pyramid,
on the highest hump of the Sierra Madre,
knocking on the sky,
on the gates of heaven,
upon the breast of God,
for a slice of light.

            .   .   .

This is my word.
And yours, also.
The old word of all the poets of the world,
of all the poets of the world,

(con el signo épico y activo que aquí homos dado a
   la palabra y al oficio).
No es la palabra de los demagogos.
¿Soy yo un demagogo?
Yo no hablo a los españoles de felicidad,
sino de heroísmo.
Y digo también:
yo no conduzco a los hombres
ni al restaurante
ni a la biblioteca
ni a la Bolsa...
Los llevo hacia esas cumbres altas.

LEON FELIPE

Drop a Star

¿Dónde está la estrella de los Nacimientos?
La tierra, encabritada, se ha parado en el viento.
Y no ven los ojos de los marineros.
Aquel pez—¡seguidle!—
se lleva, danzando,
la estrella polar.

El mundo es una slot-machine,
con una ranura en la frente del cielo,
sobre la cabecera del mar.
(Se ha parado la máquina,
se ha acabado la cuerda).
El mundo es algo que funciona
como el piano mecánico de un bar.
(Se ha acabado la cuerda,
se ha parado la máquina...)
                    Marinero,
tú tienes una estrella en el bolsillo...
                    ¡Drop a star!
Enciende con tu mano la nueva música del mundo,
la canción marinera de mañana,

(with the epic and active sign that here we've given to
    the word and the craft).
It isn't the word of demagogues.
Am I a demagogue?
I'm not speaking to Spaniards of happiness,
but of heroism.
I say, also:
I don't lead men
to the restaurant
or to the library
or to the Stock Exchange...
I take them towards those high summits.

LEON FELIPE

Drop a Star

Where is the star of Nativities?
The earth, lurching upward, has stopped in the wind.
And the eyes of the sailors do not see.
That fish—follow it!—
is carrying away, dancing,
the polar star.

The world is a *slot machine*,
with a slit in face of the sky,
above the source of the sea.
(The machine has stopped,
it's wound down).
The world is something that works
like the player piano in a bar.
(It's wound down,
the machine has stopped...)
                Sailor,
you've got a star in your pocket...
                Drop a star!
Start up this new music of the world with your hand,
this mariner's song of tomorrow,

el himno venidero de los hombres...
                    ¡Drop a star!
Echa a andar otra vez este barco varado, marinero.
Tú tienes una estrella en el bolsillo...
una estrella nueva de paladio, de fósforo y de imán.

LEON FELIPE

Madrid, Frente de Lucha

Tarde negra, lluvia y fango,
tranvías y milicianos.
Por la calzada, un embrollo
de carritos sin caballos,
o jumentos con el mísero
ajuar de los aldeanos.
Caras sin color que emigran
de los campos toledanos;
niños, viejos,
mujeres que fueron algo,
que fueron la flor del pueblo,
y hoy son la flor del harapo.
Nadie habla. Todos van,
todos vamos
a la guerra, o por la guerra,
en volandas, o rodando
a millares, como hojas
en el otoño dorado.
Pasan camiones de guerra
y filas de milicianos
entre zonas de silencio,
lluvia y fango.
Pasan banderines rojos,
delirantes, desflecados,
como nuncios de victoria
en las proas de los autos
mientras las mjeres hacen
"colas" por leche, garbanzos,
carbón, lentejas y pan.

114

this coming hymn of man...
                    Drop a star!
Sailor, start this beached ship moving again.
You've got a star in your pocket...
a new star of palladium, phosphorus and magnet.

                                        LEON FELIPE

Madrid, Battlefront

Black afternoon, rain and mire,
streetcars and militiamen.
On the causeway, a tangle
of little carts without horses,
or donkeys with the villagers'
wretched household effects.
Colorless faces that are emigrating
from the fields of Toledo;
children, old people,
women who were once something,
who were the flower of their village,
and today are a flower of tatters.
Nobody talks. They all are going,
we all are going
off to war, or through the war,
carried by the wind or tumbling
along by the thousands, like leaves
in some golden autumn.
War trucks and ranks
of militiamen pass by
amid these zones of silence,
rain and mire.
Red pennants pass by,
delirious, tattered,
like harbingeres of victory
on the bows of autos
while the women form
"lines" for milk, garbanzos,
coal, lentils and bread.

115

Los suelos están sembrados
de cristales y las casas
ya no tienen ojos claros
sino cavernas heladas,
huecos trágicos.
Hay rieles del tranvía
como cuernos levantados,
hay calles acordonadas
donde el humo hace penachos,
y hay barricadas de piedra
donde antes nos sentábamos
a mirar el cielo terso
de este Madrid confiado
abierto a todas las brisas
y sentimientos humanos.
Confundido, como pez
en globo de agua, deshago
mis pisadas por las calles.
Subo, bajo,
visito las estaciones
del Metro. Allí, como sacos,
duermen familias sin casas.
Huele a establo;
se respira malamente.
Subo, salgo.
Vuelvo a la tarde nublada.
Me siento como encerrado
en un Madrid hecho isla,
solo, en un cielo de asfalto,
por donde cruzan los cuervos
que buscan niños y ancianos.
Tarde negra; lluvia, lluvia,
tranvías y milicianos.

JOSE MORENO VILLA

The ground is sown
with glass and the houses
no longer have clear eyes,
but rather frozen caverns,
tragic cavities.
There are streetcar rails
like upraised horns,
there are cordoned-off streets
where smoke forms into tufts,
and there are stone barricades
where before we would sit down
and look at the bright sky
of this entrusting Madrid,
open to all the breezes
and human sentiments.
Confused, like a fish
in a bowl of water, I wear out
my footsteps in the streets.
Back and forth,
I visit the Metro stations.
There, like sacks,
sleep homeless families.
It smells like a stable;
one breathes poorly.
I go up and out.
I return to the cloudy afternoon.
I feel like I am enclosed
in a Madrid made into an island,
alone, in an asphalt sky
where the crows seeking out
children and old folks cross.
Black afternoon; rain, rain,
streetcars and militiamen.

JOSE MORENO VILLA

Ciudad Eterna
(Madrid 1937)

Menos dura la piedra
al ímpetu constante del tiempo que la empuja:
que la transforma lentamente en rosa,
en raíz más oculta,
en más alta montaña,
en escombro sin suerte
o acaso, con la rama, en débil voz del aire,
se inclina o se pronuncia
o invisible en su lenta forma cae.
Menos dura la piedra
a sumisión se rinde.
Menos dura la piedra
también sin dolor nace.

Triste, muy triste entraña
la que sin fuego gime.
Feliz honor el llanto
si en honra se derrama.

Feliz tú que has sabido,
aunque el dolor te insiste,
renacer de tu asedio
sin que muerta te crucen.
Más viva está tu frente
que la luz que te inunda:
de una herida en el timepo levantan tus caminos.

Ciudad, tú, ya en el sueño,
tienes parte escogida
donde tu fortaleza revistes con tus hábitos.
Pisas ya con tu gloria la tierra persistente
donde el hombre descansa, del día, por lo eterno.
Está viva tu carne si yo duermo en la guerra.
Si duerme el cielo humano,
brilla también tu sangre.

Eternal City
(Madrid 1937)[3]

Less hard the stone
with the constant violence of time pushing upon it:
transforming it slowly into rose,
into more hidden root,
into higher mountain,
into luckless rubble,
or perhaps, with the branch, into weak voice of the air,
it bends or pronounces,
or it falls, invisible in its sluggish form.
Less hard the stone,
into submission it's rendered.
Less hard the stone,
also painlessly it's born.

Sad, very sad essence
is the one that moans without fire.
Joyous honor is the lament,
if with honor it resounds.

Joyous are you who knew how,
though the pain persists,
to be reborn from your siege
without, once dead, being entered.
More alive is your visage
than the light flooding down on you:
out of these wounds, in time, will arise your roads.

City, you, already in this dream,
have a site chosen
where you will readorn your stronghold with your old habits.
Now you tread with your glory upon this persistent earth
where man rests, by day, for eternity.
Your flesh is alive even if I were to sleep in the war.
If the humane sky does sleep,
your blood, too, will shine.

Así nace la Historia;
así mueren también los inútiles ecos.
Es un lago profundo este espacio en la vida,
y el cuerpo que en él hunda
renacerá en sus ondas.

En él, tú misma existes, altiva, permanente;
que allí tu pie pusiste ya con planeta interna,
doble en tu resistencia
dentro y fuera del mundo que te alza.
Y tu pisar oculto
por las profundas algas que aún van desconocidas
derivando los sueños,
te presentan más libre arriba en tu equilibrio,
serena y reflejada
sobre el nivel que narra tus victorias.

¡Honor, honor a ti, Ciudad hermosa!
Menos dura la piedra que el timón de tu nave.

EMILIO PRADOS

Canto a la Libertad

I

No alcanzaréis su estirpe con vuestra torpe mano:
la Libertad del hombre está más alta que la soberbia
*   ciega*
como lo está la luz mucho más que la sombra en los
bosques inmensos.

Y su historia,
es la historia del propio crecimiento del hombre,
como curso del propio movimiento del río hacia la
*   mar profunda,*
como labio que aprende con esfuerzo a ordenar su
*   primera palabra,*
frenética, difícil, insaciable.

In that way History is born;
also in that way useless echoes die.
It's a profound lake, this interval of life,
and the corpse that sinks down into it
will be reborn upon its waves.

In it you yourself exist, lofty, permanent;
for there you placed your foot, now with an internal planet,
your resistance doubled
inside and outside of the world that hoists you up.
And your secret trampling
through the profound algae that still, unrecognizably,
go about making dreams drift,
appear freer to you up above in your equilibrium,
serene and reflected
above the level that recounts your victories.

Honor, honor to you, beautiful City!
Less hard the stone than the rudder of your ship.

EMILIO PRADOS

Song to Freedom

I

None of you will attain its lineage with your clumsy hand:
the Freedom of man is loftier than blind
    arrogance
just as light is greater than shadow in the
    immense forests.

And its history
is the history of the very growth of man,
like the course of the river's very movement towards the
    deep sea,
like lips learning with effort to put together its
    first frenzied,
difficult and insatiable word.

II

*Ha sido necesario que se derrumben años como
   maderas mohosas,
que se hayan muerto padres de abuelos y de nietos
   que nos antecedieron.
Ha sido necesario que los trabajadores de otras
   tierras más o menos calientes que las nuestras,
más o menos pobladas de encinas o de chopos o de
   abetos o de robles,
caigan no sólo muertos, sí ultrajados a vivos
   centenares de humillación y llanto
para que Tú amanezcas tan valerosamente por
   España,
por los lugares esos que conozco.*

*Y ha sido necesario que los hombres conquisten la
   muerte preferible
como extraño terreno y enemigo palmo a palmo,
para que Tú despiertes purísima en los labios con
   merecido nombre,
con dulces letras nuevas como gotas de miel,
   resucitada,
cuando apenas la lengua te pronunciaba entera por
   no hallar a la sombra de tu letra pasiva
desgaste falso y frío de mármol manejado tan
   miserablemente.*

¡Oh pura y blanquísima!

III

*Podéis, podéis sembrar de piedras su camino.
Podéis hostilizarla con el oscuro fango cenegoso que
   lleváis en el pecho y en vuestros ojos bajos
y podéis arrancaros de cólera los labios hartos de
   maldición inútilmente:
no alcanzaréis su estirpe con vuestra torpe mano.*

IV

*Allí donde está el hombre está la muerte.
Donde habita la sangre habita el frío, la peligrosa
   muerte de los hombres.*

II

It was necessary that years tumble down
   like moldy wood,
that fathers of grandfathers and grandchildren
   who preceeded us die.
It was necessary that workers from other
   lands, more or less as warm as ours,
more or less covered with oak trees or black poplars or
   firs or holm oaks,
fall down not only dead, even insulted with hundreds
   of cutting humiliations and laments
so You are able to dawn so courageously throughout
   Spain,
upon those places I know.

And it was necessary that men conquer this
   preferable death
inch by inch, like a strange enemy and terrain,
so You can awake so purely upon the lips with
   a deserved name,
with sweet new letters like drops of honey,
   resurrected,
when the tongue was scarcely able to pronounce You entirely
   for not encountering the shadow of your passive letters
cold and false attrition of such wretchedly handled
   marble.

Oh, purest and whitest one!

III

You can, all of you can sow its route with stones.
You can harass it with that obscure miry muck
   you carry around in your breast and lowered eyes
and you can senselessly wrench rage from those lips
   fed up with curses:
none of you will attain its lineage with your clumsy hand.

IV

There where man is, death is.
Where blood inhabits, cold inhabits, that so perilous
   death for men.

Pero Tú estás más alta porque en la muerte habitas
y en la vida también de tarde en tarde vertiginosamente
    permaneces.

Pero Tú estás más alta porque nada te hiere,
porque nada alcanza para herirte.

Tú estás en lo más alto.
Tu voz habla en la voz de los trabajadores tan dura
    en su faena
y en sus ojos Tú eres una promesa lenta como un
    buey de labor,
como campos de pan movidos por el viento en las
    praderas
que se merece siempre y cada día.

¡Eres el pabellón de triunfo colocado en lo más
    admirable del esfuerzo del hombre,
en la parte más alta que al hombre pertenece!

V

¿Pero quiénes son libres si no son los pastores?
¿Quiénes son hombres libres sino los opulentos?
¿Quiénes serán los libres si no lo son los sabios y
    poetas?

No. No alcanzaréis su estirpe con vuestra torpe mano.
No seréis hombres libres si no sois libres todos y en
    peligro de muerte.

No seréis hombres libres si no habéis paseado con
    dolor entre ruinas
sintiendo cómo nace del escombro otra vida,
tocando corazones que laten: camarada,
viniendo a firmes pulsos hace ya tiempo sueltos que
    a muerte se proclaman con títulos varones.

VI

Y por fin la alegría.
¡Venid ojos y ved! ¡Escuchad los oídos!

But You are loftier because You inhabit death
and once in a while You also vertiginously remain
    in life.

But You are loftier because nothing wounds You,
because nothing can reach You to wound You.

You are in the loftiest of places.
Your voice speaks with the voice of workers, so hardened
    in their toil,
and in their eyes You are a promise, slow like a
    beast of burden,
like grain fields moved by the wind upon the
    grasslands
that is deserved each day and always.

You are the colors of triumph placed upon the most
    admirable of man's efforts,
in the loftiest place belonging to man!

V

But who are the free if not the herdsmen?
Who are free men but the affluent ones?
Who will be the free if not wisemen and
    poets?

No. None of you will attain its lineage with your clumsy hand.
None of you will be free men if all of you are not free and
    in peril of death.

None of you will be free men if you have not strolled among
    the ruins in pain
feeling how another life is born from the rubble,
touching hearts that are beating: comrade,
becoming strong heartbeats already for some time separated
    they proclaim themselves unto death with manly headlines.

VI

And finally our joy.
Come, eyes, and see! Listen, ears!

Y las lenguas hablad ese lenguaje tan puramente
    oculto que nos mueve a movernos.

Hablad, hablad al mundo.
Hablad a las naciones que nos miran.
Dirigíos al hombre que medite en la muerte.
Venid, venid que os enseñemos:

Aquí la ciudad rota, las casas destrozadas y las calles
    funestas escombreras.
Aquí las avenidas pobladas de la muerte.
Aquí los habitantes que han perdido sus hijos o sus
    padres, sus hombres o mujeres.

Venid, venid hacia nosotros y nos conoceréis como
    nosotros os conoceremos: nuestros brazos esperan
    abiertos.
Compartid con nosotros el refugio y el pan.
Venid, venid hacia nosotros y olvidaréis lo triste
porque ya no hay tristeza entre nosotros sino
    profundo duelo, patética alegría.
Los hombres y mujeres que otros tiempos amaron
    sus sórdidos hogares
hoy duermen y descansan en otro parecido pero más
    camarada,
hoy comen de otro pan tan tiernamente blanco pero
    más solidario
porque puebla la muerte nuestra ciudad con furia.

Y
por esa muerte oscura que acompaña tan intrincada,
    terca y duramente
los hombres y mujeres son otra vez el Hombre
por obra de la muerte colectiva.

Y se olvida el recor como se olvida el hijo para vivir
    muriendo libremente,
y se olvida la sórdida querella matrimonial y oscura
como la oscura lenta y apacible tranquilidad burguesa.

¡Oh júbilo gozoso del peligro en tu nombre!

And tongues: speak that so purely hidden
    language that moves us to movement.

Speak, speak to the world.
Speak to all the nations observing us.
Address yourselves to the man who meditates upon death.
Come, come and we will show you:

Here the broken city, the houses destroyed and the streets,
    fatal rubble heaps.
Here, the avenues populated with death.
Here, the inhabitants who have lost their children or their
    parents, their men or their women.

Come towards us and know us as
    we will know you: our open arms
    await you.
Share bread and refuge with us.
Come, come towards us and forget all that is sad
for now there is not sadness between us but rather
    profound grief, pathetic joy.
Men and women who at other times loved
    their squalid homes
today rest and sleep in similar ones but with more
    comradeship,
today eat another so tenderly white bread but
    with more solidarity
for death furiously populates our city.

And
owing to that obscure death that so complicatedly, stubbornly
    and severly accompanies them
men and women are once again Man
by reason of that collective death.

And rancor is forgotten the way one's son is forgotten in order
    to live and die freely,
and the sordid matrimonial dispute is forgotten and obscured
like the obscure, slow and placid tranquillity of the bourgeoisie.

Oh, joyful jubilation of the peril in your name!

VII

No, no. Nunca.
No alcanzaréis su estirpe con vuestra torpe mano.

Mueran los sentimientos filiales y paternos.
Destrúyanse los pueblos durante tanto tiempo
   trabajados
y arruínense las calles y edificios con ira sorda y
   ciega.

Muera el amor también,
muera el amor privado como la propiedad privada
   odiosamente
y enciéndanse los ojos de contemplarte pura, de
   comprobarte excelsa
moviendo corazones de frenético vuelo.

Ni piedra sobra piedra quede,
pero Tú, con nosotros:
¡Eternamente viva sobre la muerte nuestra libre y
   merecida!

Madrid, diciembre 1936.

ARTURO SERRANO PLAJA

Primero de Mayo

I

No hay descanso ni paz en esta tierra,
en esta amarga calle señalada,
en estos corazones.
A vosotros, canteros y pastores,
obreros de París, de Londres y del mundo:
¡No hay descanso ni paz en esta tierra!

No, no. Never.
None of you will attain its lineage with your clumsy hand.

Let filial and paternal sentiments die.
Let the towns worked for such a long time
    be destroyed
and let streets and buildings be ruined in a deaf and blind
    rage.

Let love also die,
let private love die like private property
    hatefully
and let eyes light up to contemplate You as pure, to
    confirm You sublime
moving hearts of frenetic flights.

Let not stone upon stone be left,
but You, with us:
Eternally alive above our free and deserved
    death!

Madrid, December 1936.

ARTURO SERRANO PLAJA

First of May

I

There is neither rest nor peace in this land,
on this bitter and marked street,
in these hearts.
You, stonecutters and herdsmen,
workers of Paris, London and the world:
There is neither rest nor peace in this land!

II

Hombres, trabajadores lo mismo que vosotros,
con yuntas de bueyes iguales que los vuestros.
Con tornos parecidos
o con rebaños llenos también de polvo y de romero,
por el mismo cielo común y parecidas fábricas,
caminan y trabajan infatigablemente.

III

Hombres, trabajadores lo mismo que vosotros,
con hijos tan hermosos
y sábanas tan pobres en lechos parecidos,
y tierno pan, tan oloroso como el vuestro,
pelean y triunfan al pie de los olivos,
en los trigales rubios,
sobre la nieve vieja que duerme entre los pinos.
Bajo un cielo varón, hombres varones,
fuertes y alegres como lo sois vosotros,
dejan en el olvido
el incendio de sus dormitorios y abuelos mutilados.
¡No hay descanso ni paz en esta tierra
que para siempre ha de llamarse España!
Porque somos, hemos de ser, los únicos propietarios
    del día.
Dueños de las ciudades y verdaderos amos de los
    campos.

IV

Los hombres de las minas.
Los que trabajan en ganados y montes.
Los que hacen el pan y los que lo cultivan.
Los poetas, herreros, leñadores,
el nombre guardan, y la sangre del pueblo
en la quemada tierra de las avanzadillas,
en los talleres.

V

¡No hay descanso ni paz en esta tierra!
Sólo hay flores que viven en tinajas quemadas.

130

II

Men, workers the same as you,
with teams of oxen the same as yours.
With similar lathes
or with herds also covered in dust and rosemary,
across the same common sky and in similar factories,
they travel and work tirelessly.

III

Men, workers the same as you,
with such beautiful children
and such poor sheets upon similar beds,
and tender bread, as fragrant as yours,
they fight and triumph at the foot of the olive trees,
in the blond wheat fields,
upon the old snow that sleeps among the pines.
Beneath a masculine sky, masculine men,
strong and joyous as you yourselves are,
letting the burning of their bedrooms
and mutilated grandparents pass into oblivion.
There is neither rest nor peace in this land
that is forever to be called Spain!
Because we are, we must be, the sole proprietors
   of the day.
Owners of the cities and the true masters of the
   fields.

IV

The men of the mines.
Those who work with cattle and upon mountains.
Those who make the bread and those who cultivate it.
Poets, blacksmiths, woodcutters,
those names they keep, and also the people's blood
on the burnt earth of their outposts,
in their workshops.

V

There is neither rest nor peace in this land!
There are only flowers that live in burnt earthen jars.

131

Cartas que terminó la Artillería.
Hombres que no descansan,
despiertos siempre, como están los castaños
hasta que la victoria da los frutos.

Madrid, 1.º de mayo 1937.

Lorenzo Varela

Letters that the Artillery finishes.
Men who never rest,
forever awake, as are the chestnuts,
until victory produces its fruits.

(Madrid, 1st of May, 1937).

LORENZO VARELA

HOMENAJE
DE DESPEDIDA
A LAS BRIGADAS
INTERNACIONALES

Palabras de ANTONIO MACHADO; Versos de
RAFAEL ALBERTI, MANUEL ALTOLAGUIRRE,
PEDRO GARFIAS, JUAN GIL-ALBERT, MIGUEL
HERNÁNDEZ, JOSÉ HERRERA PETERE, PABLO
NERUDA, JUAN PAREDES, PÉREZ INFANTE,
EMILIO PRADOS, ARTURO SERRANO PLAJA
y LORENZO VARELA

EDICIONES ESPAÑOLAS

Farewell Homage to the
International Brigades

If there is one thing the people of Republican Spain will never forget, it is how men from all over the world came to their aid. Men from some fifty-three countries overcame every barrier to get to Spain, whether political barriers their own governments tried to impose or the difficulties of the trek across the Pyrenees. Of the 35,000 or so men who fought in the International Brigades, some came merely with the clothes on their backs, while others—many of whom had fought in World War I—brought anything that might be useful, from pistols and binoculars to motorcycles. But all of them brought their love of freedom and justice.

In this volume we have the feeling of the Spanish people towards the Brigades; for example, the poem of Rafael Alberti. We have poems about the dead they left behind: those of Manuel Altolaguirre, Miguel Hernández and José Herrera Petere. Pablo Neruda's poem articulates the feelings of the people of Madrid on seeing the first Brigades arrive. And the feeling of loss when the International Brigades were to leave finds expression in the poem of Serrano Plaja.

The words of the poet Antonio Machado, from the original introduction, summarize the feelings of helplessness and hopelessness in the face of geopolitical factors: "... our best friends are to abandon us, those generous and sacrificing men...who have fought for an ideal of justice and an authentic Spain....

"They—those volunteers *par excellence*—are leaving because the very highest reasons of state demanded it.

"With their absence, in fact, there is something that no one can put in doubt. Spain struggles on alone, completely alone, against this foreign invasion...."

A las Brigadas Internacionales

Venís desde muy lejos... Mas esta lejanía,
¿qué es para vuestra sangre, que canta sin fronteras?
La necesaria muerte os nombra cada día,
no importa en qué ciudades, campos o carreteras.

De este país, del otro, del grande, del pequeño,
del que apenas si al mapa da un color desvaído,
con las mismas raíces que tiene un mismo sueño,
sencillamente anónimos y hablando habéis venido.

No conocéis siquiera ni el color de los muros
que vuestro infranqueable compromiso amuralla.
La tierra que os entierra la defendéis, seguros,
a tiros con la muerte vestida de batalla.

Quedad, que así lo quieren los árboles, los llanos,
las mínimas partículas de la luz que reanima
un solo sentimiento que el mar sacude: ¡Hermanos!
Madrid con vuestro nombre se agranda y se ilumina.

RAFAEL ALBERTI

Homenaje a los Americanos Muertos en Defensa de España

Una muerte española, el mar en medio,
desde una hermosa vida americana
vino a nacer aquí a los jardines
donde los héroes niños permanecen.
La juventud de América caída
enriqueció la tierra con su sangre,
con sus perennes huesos no besados.

To the International Brigades

You've come from very far away... But this distance,
what could it mean to your blood that sings without frontiers?
Each day this so necessary death claims you,
it doesn't matter whether in cities, fields or on roads.

From this country, from another, from a large one, a small one,
from one that scarcely produces a pallid color on the map,
with the same roots that have a similar dream,
you simply came, anonymous and conversing.

You didn't even know the color of the walls
your insurmountable commitment fortifies.
The earth that will bury you, you defend, confident,
with bullets against a death dressed for battle.

Remain, for the trees, the plains, the minute particles
of light, that reanimate one lone sentiment
which is tossed about by the sea, want it that way: Brothers!
Madrid is aggrandized and brightened with your name.

RAFAEL ALBERTI

Homage to the Americans Killed in Defense of Spain

A Spanish death, the sea in the middle,
came here from a beautiful American life
to give birth to the gardens
where the child heroes remain.
The fallen youth of America
enriched the earth with its blood,
with its perennial, unkissed bones.

Sobre esa superficie y apariencia,
sobre esa destrucción asimilada,
crecen en la memoria trascendente,
con la misma inocencia que los niños,
los invisibles huéspedes hermanos.
Son mis muertos de un mes, de cuatro meses,
los que cumplen un año, los que pueden
andar y sonreír, decir palabras,
los que abrazan a la antigua madre
y juegan en su sol, junto a sus ríos.

Eran hombres, murieron en la guerra,
hoy son niños de niebla en el recuerdo,
juegan en esta orilla del Atlántico
sobre una playa gris de blanca espuma.
Son un ariente beso de la historia
sobre un paisaje hermoso y ponderado.
Otra vez sobre ti, mi España bella,
la pasión, el amor, los heroísmos,
te vistieron de gloria, te dejaron
al desnudo el espíritu encendido.
Al desgarrar tu tierra concediste
obscuridad, silencio a los despojos,
luz tremolante y cálida a los cielos,
de tus heridas como sepulturas.

MANUEL ALTOLAGUIRRE

Al Soldado Internacional Caído en España

Si hay hombres que contienen un alma sin fronteras,
una esparcida frente de mundiales cabellos,
cubierta de horizontes, barcos y cordilleras,
con arena y con nieve, tú eres uno de aquellos.

Las patrias te llamaron con todos sus banderas,
que tu aliento llenara de movimientos bellos.
Quisiste apaciguar la sed de las panteras,
y flameaste henchido contra sus atropellos.

Upon that surface and appearance,
upon that assimilated destruction,
these invisible, brotherly guests,
with the same innocence as children,
grow in one's transcendent memory.
They are my one month old dead, of four months,
those who are a year old, those who can
walk and smile, say words,
those who embrace the ancient mother
and play in her sun, next to her rivers.

They were men, they died in the war,
today they are children of mist in one's remembrance,
they are playing on this edge of the Atlantic
upon a grey beach of white foam.
They are the ardent kiss of history
upon a beautiful and measured landscape.
Once again, my lovely Spain,
passion, love and heroisms
dressed you in glory, leaving
your inflamed spirit naked.
On tearing apart your land, you granted,
from your wounds that are like open graves,
darkness, silence to the remains,
a trembling and warm light to the skies.

MANUEL ALTOLAGUIRRE

To the International Soldier Fallen in Spain

If there are men who are composed of a soul without frontiers,
a forehead scattered with universal tresses,
covered with horizons, ships and mountain ranges,
with sand and with snow, then you are one of them.

Homelands called out to you with all their banners
that your life's breath was to fill with lovely movement.
You wished to calm the thirst of the panthers,
and once filled you flourished against their outrages.

139

Con un sabor a todos los soles y los mares,
España te recoge porque en ella realices
tu majestad de árbol que abarca un continente.

A través de tus huesos irán los olivares
desplegando en la tierra sus más férreas raíces,
abrazando a los hombres univesal, fielmente.

Miguel Hernandez

A Jaskel Honigstein

Ultimo Caído de las Brigadas Internacionales

Jaskel Honigstein, polaco,
obrero, judío de raza,
hijo de una tierra obscura,
muerto a la luz de mi Patria.

El pueblo rabioso grita
tu muerte a Europa en su cara.
¡Jaskel Honigstein, obrero
muerto a la luz de batalla!

Tu sangre es la última gota
de aquel torrente de lava
que de las cumbres del mundo
bajó generoso a España.

De una corriente de fuego
que las fronteras traspasa,
abrasando cobardías,
iluminando esperanzas.

¡Jaskel Honigstein, obrero
muerto a la luz del mañana!

Que los abetos se yergan
en las umbrías tierras polacas

With a taste of all the suns and seas,
Spain gathers you together, for here you were to fulfill
your tree-like majesty that takes in a continent.

The olive groves will set about piercing your bones,
unfolding their most ferrous of roots in the earth,
embracing men universally, faithfully.

MIGUEL HERNANDEZ

To Jaskel Honigstein

Last of the International Brigades' Fallen

Jaskel Honigstein, Pole,
worker, of the Jewish race,
son of a dark land,
dead in the light of my Homeland.

This enraged people shouts
your death in Europe's face.
Jaskel Honigstein, worker
dead in the light of battle!

Your blood is the last drop
of that torrent of lava
that generously descended on Spain
from the summits of the world.

From a fiery current
that crosses all boundaries,
scorching cowardices,
illuminating hopes.

Jaskel Honigstein, worker
dead in the light of tomorrow!

Let firs stand straight
in those shady Polish soils

de orgullo, como el olivo
del valle del Ebro en llamas.

Amigo: ¡Salud! del pueblo.
Salud desde la batalla.
Jaskel Honigstein, tu muerte,
que es de amor, será vengada.

JOSE HERRERA PETERE

Llegada a Madrid de la Brigada Internacional

Una mañana de un mes frío,
de un mes agonizante, manchado por el lodo y por el humo,
un mes sin rodillas, un triste mes de sitio y desventura,
cuando a través de los cristales mojados de mi casa
     se oían los chacales africanos
aullar con los rifles y los dientes llenos de sangre, entonces,
cuando no teníamos más esperanza que un sueño de pólvora,
     cuando ya creíamos
que el mundo estaba lleno sólo de monstruos devoradores
     y de furias,
entonces, quebrando la escarcha del mes de frío en Madrid,
     en la niebla,
del alba
he visto con estos ojos que tengo, con este corazón que mira,
he visto llegar a los claros, a los dominadores combatientes
de la delgada y dura y madura y ardiente brigada de piedra.

Era el acongojado tiempo en que las mujeres
llevaban una ausencia como un carbón terrible,
y la muerte española, más ácida y aguda que otras muertes,
llenaba los campos hasta entonces honrados por el trigo.

Por las calles la sangre rota del hombre se juntaba
con el agua que sale del corazón destruído de las casas;

of pride, like the olive tree
of the Ebro Valley in flames.

My friend: *Salud!*[1] from the people.
Salud from the battle lines.
Jaskel Honigstein, your death,
which comes from love, will be avenged.

JOSE HERRERA PETERE

Arrival in Madrid of the International Brigade

One morning of a cold month,
of a dying month, stained with mire and smoke,
a kneeless month, a sad month of siege and misfortune,
when through the wet windows of my house
   the African jackals were to be heard
howling with rifles and their teeth dripping with blood, then,
when we didn't have any hope other than a gunpowder dream,
   when already we believed
that the world was filled only with devouring monsters
   and with rages,
then, breaking through the frost of that cold month in Madrid,
   in the fog
of that dawn
I saw with these eyes I have, with this heart that observes,
I saw arriving those clear, those dominating combatants
of that thin and hard and mature and ardent brigade of stone.

It was an anguishing time when women
carried an absence around with them like some terrible coal,
and this Spanish death, sharper and more acid than other deaths,
filled fields up till then honored by wheat.

Through the streets the broken blood of man would join
with the water flowing from the destroyed heart of houses;

los huesos de los niños deshechos, el desgarrador
enlutado silencio de las madres, los ojos
cerrados para siempre de los indefensos
eran como la tristeza y la pérdida, eran como un jardín escupido,
eran la fe y la flor asesinada para siempre.

Camaradas,
entonces
os he visto,
y mis ojos están hasta ahora llenos de orgullo
porque os vi a través de la mañana de niebla
    llegar a la frente pura de Castilla
silenciosos y firmes
como campanas antes del alba,
llenos de solemnidad y de ojos azules venir de lejos y lejos,
venir de vuestros rincones, de vuestras patrias perdidas,
    de vuestros sueños
llenos de dulzura quemada y de fusiles
a defender la ciudad española en que la libertad acorralada
pudo caer y morir mordida por las bestias.

Hermanos, que desde ahora
vuestra pureza y vuestra fuerza, vuestra historia solemne
sea conocida del niño y del varón, de la mujer y del viejo,
llegue a todos los seres sin esperanza, baje a las minas
    corroídas por el aire sulfúrico,
suba las escaleras inhumanas del esclavo,
que todas las estrellas, que todas las espigas de Castilla
    y del mundo
escriban vuestro nombre y vuestra áspera lucha
y vuestra victoria fuerte y terrestre como una encina roja.

Porque habéis hecho renacer con vuestro sacrificio
la fe perdida, el alma ausente, la confianza en la tierra,
y por vuestra abundancia, por vuestra nobleza,
    por vuestros muertos,
como por un valle de duras rocas de sangre
pasa un inmenso río con palomas de acero y de esperanza.

PABLO NERUDA

144

the bones of torn-apart children, the heart-rending,
grief-filled silence of mothers, the eyes
of defenseless ones forever shut,
were like sadness and loss, were like a spit-upon garden,
were faith and flower murdered for all time.

Comrades,
then
I saw you,
and even now my eyes are filled with pride
because I saw you, through that foggy morning,
    arriving at the pure visage of Castile,
silent and resolute
like bells before the dawn,
filled with solemnity and blue eyes, coming from far, far away,
coming from those far corners, from your lost homelands,
    from your dreams
filled with a burnt sweetness and guns
to defend this Spanish city where an intimidated freedom
could fall and die, chewed apart by those beasts.

Brothers, from now on
may your purity and your strength, your solemn history
be known by the child and the man, by the woman and the old man,
may it reach all beings without hope, descend into the mines
    corroded by sulphuric air,
climb the inhuman staircases of the slave,
may all the stars, may all the wheat shoots of Castile
    and the world
write down your name and your bitter struggle
and your victory, strong and terrestrial like a red oak.

Because of your sacrifice you have made lost faith,
absent soul, confidence in the earth, be reborn,
and through your abundance, through your nobleness,
    through your dead,
as if through a valley of hard rocks made of blood,
flows an immense river with doves of steel and hope.

PABLO NERUDA

A los Voluntarios Internacionales
(Despedida)

Adiós, hermanos nuestros.

Locomotoras tristes os esperan
con un sonido ronco en los andenes,
y muerden las sirenas de los buques
el aire palpitante de los puertos
con desgarrado llanto y os reclaman.

Subid, subid a bordo.

Sois dignos de los mares, hombres puros.
Los viejos marineros os saludan,
desde su grave estirpe concentrada
en horas de remotos sufrimientos
y abandonado tedio navegante,
con encendido orgullo en la pupila.

Subid, subid a bordo.

España os ve partir hacia otros mundos
como esas madres nuestras que os han visto
con una oculta pena entre pañuelos
y mantones de luto, gravemente,
desde la pobre puerta de su casa,
partir hacia el combate a defenderlas.
Adiós, adiós, hermanos,
nobles hermanos nuestros en la sangre.

Vosotros, alemanes perseguidos,
demócratas noruegos de ojos claros,
checoslovacos puros,
austriacos desterrados hace tiempo.
Vosotros los franceses
de atropellado júbilo impetuosos,
los chinos de impasible

To the International Volunteers
(Farewell)

Goodbye, our brothers.

Sad locomotives await you
at the platforms with a harsh sound,
and the ships' sirens bite into
the palpitating air of the ports
with a heart-rending lament and they reclaim you.

Climb, climb aboard.

You are worthy of the seas, pure men.
The ancient mariners salute you,
from their grave, introspective lineage
in hours of remote sufferings
and the abandoned tedium of navigation,
with an ardent pride in their pupils.

Climb, climb aboard.

Spain sees you departing toward other worlds
like those mothers of ours who saw you,
with a hidden sorrow amid handkerchiefs
and shawls of mourning, gravely,
from that poor door of their houses,
leaving for combat to defend them.
Goodbye, goodbye, brothers,
noble brothers of ours in the blood.

You, pursued Germans,
democratic Norwegians of clear eyes,
pure Czechoslovakians,
Austrians for some time now exiled.
You, Frenchmen,
impetuous ones of trampled joy,
Chinamen of impassible

147

y apretado calor de independencia.
Los que enarbolan, dignos de Inglaterra,
su nombre y apellido aquí en España,
dignamente luchando,
muriendo libremente.

Y vosotros también los italianos,
los que no sometidos, combatiendo,
claváis el pabellón de vuestra Italia,
venerable y antigua,
frente al triste rebaño degollado.

Y vosotros, polacos,
búlgaros y daneses clandestinos,
belgas, suizos o griegos,
humillados judíos,
hombre que habéis venido atravesando
fronteras para pobres,
barreras y montañas y países
que oponen sus guardianes cancerberos
a vuestra sed sin puertas,
a vuestra frente limpia,
a vuestro corazón esclarecido,
escuchad, habla España.

Escuchadla, vosotros
y vosotros también, hermanos nuestros
legítimos de sangre y de mirada,
hijos del continente americano,
hombres libres de América del Norte,
mexicanos purísimos de raza,
mulatos despreciados
y negros ofendidos.

Y vosotros, cubanos, y vosotros
argentinos con viento de la pampa,
callados uruguayos,
maltratados chilenos.
Todos, todas las razas,
todos los pueblos, todos
los claros corazones verdaderos,
los que han sufrido penas y amarguras,

and gripping ardor for independence.
Those who hoist up, worthy of their England,
their first and last names here in Spain,
honorably fighting,
freely dying.

And you Italians, also,
those not subjugated, locked in combat,
driving in that banner of your Italy,
venerable and ancient,
in the face of that sad, decapitated herd.

And you, Poles,
Bulgarians and clandestine Danes,
Belgians, Swiss or Greeks,
humiliated Jews,
men who came by crossing
frontiers for the poor,
barriers and mountains and countries
whose Cerberus-like guardians oppose
your unbounded thirst,
your clear brow,
your noble heart,
listen, Spain speaks.

Listen to her, you
and you, also, brothers of ours,
genuine in blood and gaze,
sons of the American continent,
free men of North America,
Mexicans, the very purest of their race,
despised mulattoes
and offended Negroes.

And you, Cubans, and you,
Argentineans with the wind of the Pampa,
silenced Uruguayans,
ill-treated Chileans.
All, all the races,
all the peoples, all
the clear, true hearts,
those who have suffered sorrows and bitterness,

los que llevan su historia en su mirada,
todos habéis pisado nuestra tierra.

Habéis sido el asombro solidario
de nuestros pobres pueblos silenciosos.
Habeís montado guardia en las aldeas,
habéis partido el pan con nuestros niños
y habéis vertido la sangre con nosotros.

Y España. ¿Qué os ha dado?
Tristeza polvorienta en los caminos,
amarga soledad, melancolía,
barro mordido, piojos,
y un sonido de pólvora en los montes,
de cólera en los llanos,
de rabia calcinada en las ciudades.

Y además os ofrece
—por eso sois hermanos—
un orgullo profundo,
una piedad templada, de varones,
una crecida muerte, como un toro
que calma su poder en su agonía:
¡La muerte merecida en la batalla!

ARTURO SERRANO PLAJA

150

those who carry their history in their gaze,
all of you have trod our land.

You were that astonishing solidarity
for our poor and silent towns.
You stood guard in the villages,
you broke bread with our children
and you shed your blood alongside us.

And Spain? What has she given you?
Dusty sadness on the roads,
bitter solitude, melancholy,
chewed mud, lice,
and a sound of gunpowder in the hills,
of anger on the plains,
of calcinated rage in the cities.

And she also offers you
—for that you are brothers—
a profound pride,
a tempered compassion, of men,
and an ample death, like a bull
when he quiets his power in his agony:
A death deserved in battle!

ARTURO SERRANO PLAJA

Translator's Notes

INTRODUCTION

1. Max Aub, *Campo abierto* (Madrid, 1978), p. 195.

2. Max Aub, *La poesía española contemporánea* (Mexico, 1954), p. 186.

3. Serge Salaun, "La expresión poética durante la guerra de España," Marc Hanrez, ed., *Los escritores y la guerra de España* (Barcelona, 1977), pp. 143–44.

4. Luis Cernuda, *Estudios sobre poesía española contemporánea* (Madrid, 1957), pp. 229–30.

5. Natalia Calamai, *El compromiso de la poesía en la guerra civil española* (Barcelona, 1979), p. 252.

ROMANCES OF THE CIVIL WAR (SERIES I)

1. Lina Odena is representative of a whole class of women, from Dolores Ibárruri ("La Pasionaria") to the anonymous militiawomen, who fought—and many times died—for the Spanish Republic. Sent from her native Catalonia to command the militias around Granada, Lina Odena chose death rather than surrender to Franco's Moors and *legionnaires*.

2. *Arellanos* was the name given to the troops under the command of *comandante* Eulogio Arellano. Arellano was one of a few military men from the regular army who sided with the Republic. He died a hero in defense of Madrid near the end of 1936.

3. General Emilio Mola was leader of the rebel forces in the north and one of the chief conspirators against the Republic. Many priests from Navarre went into battle with his troops.

4. Once the rebellion in Sevilla succeeded, General Gonzalo Queipo de Llano began an incredible nightly radio commentary, filled with barracks vocabulary, on the war and life in Sevilla. A heavy drinker, Queipo de Llano would ramble on and on, from what he would do to the "Reds" to bragging about the sexual feats of his Moorish troops. All this made him world famous and ardently listened to on both sides of the lines.

153

5. Málaga, Jerez, Montilla, Cazalla and Chinchón, besides being the names of towns, are also names of wines and liquors.

POETS IN LOYALIST SPAIN

1. General title which includes the following two poems by Rafael Alberti.

2. General title which includes the following two poems by Manuel **Altolaguirre.**

3. It reads *"(Madrid 1973)"* in the original.

FAREWELL HOMAGE TO THE INTERNATIONAL **BRIGADES**

1. *Salud* is the leftist farewell.

Biographical Notes

Rafael Alberti was born in Puerto de Santa María (Cádiz) in 1902. After moving to Madrid with his family in 1917, he studied art and began a career as a painter. For his book *Marinero en tierra*, he shared the 1925 *Premio Nacional de Literatura* with the poet Gerardo Diego. In 1931 he joined the Spanish Communist Party. During the Spanish Civil War Alberti was the moving force behind many cultural projects, and was one of the Republic's most prolific poets. He went into exile at the end of the war, first in France, then in Buenos Aires and finally in Rome, where he moved in 1962. In 1968 he received the Lenin Peace Prize. After Franco's death he returned to Spain and was elected to the Spanish Parliament. In 1983 Alberti was awarded the prestigious *Premio Cervantes*.

Vicente Aleixandre, born in Sevilla in 1898, spent his childhood in Málaga and in Madrid, where he lives today. Although seriously ill throughout most of the civil war, Aleixandre did join his fellow poets in giving readings of his poetry at demonstrations supporting the war effort. After the civil war he became a symbol of anti-francoist resistance for the younger poets inside Spain. His book *La destrucción o el amor* won the *Premio Nacional de Literatura* in 1935. Twice, in 1963 and 1969, he received the prestigious *Premio de la Crítica*. Aleixandre has been a member of the *Real Academia Española* since 1955. In 1977 he became the only member of the famous "Generation of 27" to win a Nobel Prize.

Manuel Altolaguirre was born in Málaga in 1905. In 1926 he founded (with Emilio Prados) one of the most important pre-war poetry magazines, *Litoral*. He also founded two other important literary magazines outside Spain: *Poesía* (in Paris) and *1616* (in London). He was awarded the 1933 *Premio Nacional de Literatura* for his book *La lenta libertad*. Altolaguirre was active in all areas during the civil war, and was one of the founders and directors of *Hora de España*. After the war he went first to Cuba and then Mexico, where he began a career in film. On returning to Spain in 1959 to present one of his films at the San Sebastián Film Festival, he was killed with his wife in an automobile accident.

José Bergamín was born in Madrid in 1895. A progressive Catholic, Bergamín edited one of the most important Spanish literary magazines of the twentieth century, *Cruz y Raya*. He also published books by Alberti and García Lorca before the war. During the war he was president of the

Council for Culture. After a short period of exile in Uruguay, he went to Mexico where he founded the publishing house Séneca. Bergamín returned to Spain in 1958, but because of his opposition to the Franco regime the government expelled him in 1963. He was able to return in 1970. Bergamín died in 1983.

Luis Cernuda was born in Sevilla in 1902. Before the war he taught at the University of Toulouse. During the war he was one of the editors of *Hora de España,* then taught at various universities in England and the United States until 1952. Prior to his death in 1963 he lived in Mexico.

León Felipe (León Felipe Camino Galicia), born in Tábara (Zamora) in 1884, spent the greater part of his life outside Spain. After studying pharmacy, and working for a time as a hospital administrator in Spanish Guinea, he became an actor. He traveled with various acting companies for several years. In 1923 he left for the United States, where he studied at Columbia University and taught at Cornell. Besides being a poet, León Felipe was also the translator of Walt Whitman. He was active in anarchist circles during the civil war. León Felipe lived in Mexico from the end of the war until his death in 1968.

Born in Alcoy (Alicante) in 1906, **Juan Gil-Albert** studied in both Valencia and France. He was one of the founders of *Hora de España,* and took part in the Congress of Anti-fascist Writers in 1937. Exiled in 1939, he was first interned in a French concentration camp, but later made his way to Mexico. There he collaborated with Octavio Paz in the magazine *Taller.* Gil-Albert returned to Spain in 1947, and today he lives in Valencia.

Miguel Hernández, born in Orihuela (Alicante), spent his first yeras herding goats. In 1934 he went to Madrid and became friends with Aleixandre and Neruda, both of whom influenced his work greatly. A member of the Spanish Communist Party, Hernández put himself at the service of the Fifth Regiment as soon as war broke out—and fought until the last days. As the Republican zone crumbled, he tried to escape to Portugal, but Salazar's police turned him over to the Spanish Civil Guard. Miguel Hernández died in the prison hospital in Alicante on March 28, 1942, despite the efforts of friends and a number of French writers to aid him. He was thirty-two years old.

José Herrera Petere was born in Guadalajara in 1910. The son of a famous Republican general, Herrera Petere studied law in Madrid. While still very young, his poetry began appearing in magazines such as *La Gaceta Literaria* and Rafael Alberti's *Octubre.* He joined the Fifth Regiment the moment civil war broke out. While at the front, he also served as war correspondent for the newspaper *Milicia Popular.* Herrera Petere's novel,

Biographical Notes

Acero de Madrid, won the *Premio Nacional de Literatura* in 1938. He escaped to France, and after a short time in the Saint-Cyprien concentration camp, made his way to Mexico. From 1947 until his death in 1977, he lived and taught in Geneva, Switzerland.

Antonio Machado, professor of French at various high schools in Spain and one of the most important poets of the twentieth century, was born in Sevilla in 1875, In 1927 he was elected to the *Real Academia Española.* Machado took an active part in the republican movements that led to the fall of the monarchy in 1931. At the outbreak of the Spanish Civil War, he declared himself unequivocally on the side of the Republic, and he worked for the Republic throughout the war. With the fall of Catalonia, he fled to France along with 400,000 other evacuees. Machado died on February 22, 1939, one month after having crossed the French border.

José Moreno Villa was born in Málaga in 1887. After studying in Madrid and Germany, he went to work for the *Centro de Estudios Históricos.* Besides being a poet, he was also a well-known painter. Both before and after the civil war Moreno Villa was a sort of older brother to many of the younger poets of the day. In 1937 the Education Ministry sent him on a cultural mission to the United States and Mexico, where he explained the plight of the Spanish Republic. The war ended while he was in Mexico, and he spent the rest of his life there, until his death in 1955.

Born Neftalí Ricardo Reyes Basoalto in Parral, Chile, in 1904, **Pablo Neruda** spent the years between 1925 and 1947 as a Chilean diplomat. In 1934 he was named Consul General in Madrid. While in Madrid he founded his famous poetry magazine, *Caballo Verde para la Poesía.* Neruda worked actively for the Spanish cause during the civil war; afterwards, he helped many thousands of Spaniards escape to America. In 1945 he was elected to the senate in Chile, and he joined the Chilean Communist Party. When the Communist Party was outlawed in 1949, Neruda himself became a political exile. In 1952 he was awarded the Lenin Peace Prize, and he won the Nobel Prize for Literature in 1971. He returned to Chile in 1953 and in 1971 was named Chilean ambassador to France. Neruda died of cancer in the wake of the coup that overthrew the Allende government in 1973.

The painter **Pascual Palacios Tardez,** whose drawing is on the cover of this book, was born in Madrid in 1920. His first years were spent in Madrid, Paris and San Sebastián. During the civil war he fought as a militiaman in the defense of Madrid, and he worked as an illustrator for the magazines *Al Ataque* and *Combate.* Palacios was active in the anti-francoist resistance inside Spain after the war. His paintings have been shown throughout the world. He now resides in Madrid.

Interested in social questions before any of his contemporaries, **Emilio Prados** (1899–1962) founded—with Manuel Altolaguirre—the magazine *Litoral* in his native Málaga. He studied at the University of Madrid and in Germany. Returning to Málaga, he spent much of his time teaching workers to read and write, and he took an active part in syndicalist organizations. During the civil war Prados worked for the radio, edited the famous *Romancero de la guerra de España* and participated in the *Altovoz del frente* (Loudspeaker of the Front) programs. He fled to France with the fall of the Republic, and then to Mexico, where he collaborated with José Bergamín in the publishing house Séneca. Prados spent the rest of his life in the Mexican capital.

Arturo Serrano Plaja was born in El Escorial in 1909. Besides being a poet, Serrano Plaja was an essayist, journalist and teacher. Before the war his poetry appeared in Neruda's *Caballo Verde para la Poesía*. He volunteered during the first days of the war, and fought until the last days. Antonio Machado called him one of the finest examples of the "soldier-poet or poet-soldier." After the war, Serrano Plaja lived in Buenos Aires, Paris and California, where he taught for a number of years at the University of California at Santa Barbara. He died in 1979.

Born in Havana, Cuba, in 1916, **Lorenzo Varela** passed his adolescence in the north of Spain, studying in Lugo. Varela was active both at the front and behind the lines during the civil war, and he was also one of the participants at the Second International Congress of Anti-fascist Writers in 1937. From 1939 until his death in 1978, Varela lived in France, Mexico and Argentina.